ONCE UPON A TIME
IN NORFOLK

T0347313

ONCE UPON A TIME IN NORFOLK

WRITTEN BY

ISABELLE KING

ILLUSTRATED BY
JOHN McKEEVER

The
History
Press

First published 2018

The History Press
The Mill, Brimscombe Port
Stroud, Gloucestershire, GL5 2QG
www.thehistorypress.co.uk

British Library Cataloguing in Publication Data.
A catalogue record for this book is available from the British Library.

ISBN 978 0 7509 8415 7

Typesetting and origination by The History Press
Printed in Great Britain

CONTENTS

Isabelle King
(Wolf Marloh Photography)

*O*nce upon a time, I visited Norfolk Collections Centre at Gressenhall Farm and Workhouse, part of the Norfolk Museums Service. As soon as I stepped inside the store, I knew that I wanted to write about it. An atmospheric cabinet of curiosities, the store was filled with unique objects all relating to Norfolk history which captivated my imagination. I went on to write *The Norfolk Story Book*, a book of seven short stories, all original works of fiction inspired by the objects in the store. I absolutely loved writing the book and I'm thrilled with the wonderfully positive response it has received from readers, including a shortlisting for the *Eastern Daily Press* People's Choice Awards for Best Individual 2017, all very exciting – and after all that, I just couldn't stop writing stories!

Growing up in Norfolk, I visited lots of Norfolk Museums Service museums which really sparked my creativity. Much like Martha in 'The Story Weavers', a story you will go on to read in this book, I've always had a wild imagination. When I was younger, it's fair to say that this shone through in a very theatrical way. I loved performing, so much so that I went on to pursue a career in acting. I started out with Norfolk Youth Music Theatre, appearing in the chorus of *The Wind in the Willows* as a singing weasel and in *Oliver!* as a crafty pickpocket – enough of a taste to know I wanted to stay on stage as much as possible.

I went on to train with the National Youth Theatre and East 15 Acting School, after which I worked professionally in theatre for several years, a career which saw me in a variety of Shakespearian guises, including Juliet in *Romeo and Juliet* with the Young Shakespeare Company and Vienna's English Theatre and Ariel in *The Tempest* in rep with the Cambridge Shakespeare Festival, in which I also played Feste the clown in *Twelfth Night* – a particular career highlight in which I juggled oranges and wore a rather striking pair of mustard yellow trousers! Never a dull moment as an actress.

But my creative flair kept pulling me home to Norfolk and the museums which inspired me as a child. What a joy it's been to soak up the atmosphere of each museum and bring its history to life through my ideas. In this book you will read stories inspired by Norwich Castle, Strangers' Hall, Elizabethan House Museum, Time and Tide Museum, Lynn Museum, Ancient House Museum, Gressenhall Farm and Workhouse and the Museum of Norwich at the Bridewell. In each story, I mix history with fiction.

Now, if I'm going to do that, it's very important that I get my facts right before I start jolly well making things up. First, I put my history hat on and get down to some research. Research is great fun; it involves asking lots of questions to the fantastically helpful curators and staff at Norfolk Museums Service and making notes in my messy yet fiercely organised notebooks. To create the setting for my story, I gather information for the era I'm going to write about, then explore the museum within that era. For example, I discovered that Norwich Castle was built as a Norman castle and this involved learning about Norman England. Following the research comes the part where I make things up, create the characters and situations, and add all the fun and imagination.

Some of the objects featured in the stories can be seen at the museums and are highlighted in this book so that you can see them for yourself. It would have been impossible to write this book without the wonderful support of the chief curator at the Norfolk Museums Service, Dr John Davies, to whom I would like to give special thanks for helping me to research the history behind each story and for reading the stories countless times to ensure they were factually correct. I would also like to give thanks to brilliant Megan Dennis, curator at Gressenhall Farm and Workhouse, who helped me to research the Workhouse story, 'Grey Skies and Silver Linings'.

I would very much like to thank all the staff at the Norfolk Museums Service for their amazing support of both this book and *The Norfolk Story Book*. Enormous thanks to my wonderful publisher, The History Press. Abundant thanks to John McKeever for bringing my ideas to life through magnificent illustrations. I would also like to thank the Prince's Trust for its support, in particular, my fantastic business mentor Clare Stammers.

Thank you to my family and friends – you guys are the best.

And now, reader, I would like to thank you – yes, you! – for reading this book, whether you're at home, in school, on a train, in a park, in a café or snuggled up in bed. Wherever you are, I hope this book takes you on a great adventure! I hope each story captivates your imagination and brings you the same delight and wonder that I experienced in writing them. And of course, I hope that these stories will inspire you to write stories of your own. Perhaps next time you visit a Norfolk Museums Service museum you could make up a story about it. Why not find out where your 'once upon a time' will take you? Now, let's get lost in some Norfolk magic!

1

ADVENTURE CASTLE

INSPIRED BY NORWICH CASTLE

In the Story – Castle Battlements,
the Great Hall and a Stone Lion Carving

Once upon a time, a very exciting time, a
time of kings, castles, knights, princesses,
magnificence, merriment, feasts, folly and
pies, lots of pies, Norwich was a very important
place to live. Norwich was a Norman town
because, at this time, the Normans had invaded
England and won a great big battle, which

meant that the kings who ruled the land were Norman kings. The town boasted one of the finest Norman castles in all the country, which made it a very powerful place and so popular that it often received a right royal visit. The Norman king at the time of this story was called Henry. We know him now as King Henry the First, a proud warrior of a king, and should you have met him, you would be sure to bow straight away or he would soon have something to say!

Now, one summer's day, a man riding a horse, a messenger of the king, galloped up to Norwich Castle and shouted at the top of his voice that King Henry was coming to visit.

'Make ready for the King! He'll be here in precisely three days. Actually, make that two, because it took me a day to get here! Actually, make that one and a half, because I stopped for a snack on the way!'

All at once there was a huge uproar of panic and excitement. A visit from the king! Make everything look the most splendid it has ever looked! Prepare food, the finest food you've ever feasted your eyes on! Most importantly, get some quality entertainment together. The king was known as rather a fun-loving sort who didn't like to be bored, not for a second. His time at Norwich Castle must be an extraordinarily enjoyable time, a time to remember, a time of great adventure.

Speaking of great adventure, let's meet the star of this story, a boy called Ralph. Ralph was the son of the chamberlain; the chamberlain was a well-to-do person who looked after the castle. Ralph was an extremely energetic thrill-seeker of a boy, adventure in his eyes, adventure on his mind – the most adventurous boy anyone had ever seen, if, that is, they could see him at all. You see, Ralph was seldom visible. Sometimes he was up, high in a tree, swinging through branches, climbing up walls, dangling from ceilings. Sometimes he was down, hiding under a table, behind a tapestry or crouched in a corner ready to pounce into action. Sometimes he was all around, popping up in unexpected places and making people jump, whizzing and whirring about. Blink and you missed him.

It was just as well that Ralph enjoyed being super active because, as the chamberlain's son, he was expected to learn fighting and swordsmanship, a boisterous activity at which he excelled, and it gave him the perfect opportunity to play his favourite game, pretending to be a knight. He called himself 'Ralph the Ready, Ready for Adventure!'

The only time Ralph was not bouncing about like a spring on the loose was when he attended his lessons. Ralph was taught reading, writing and languages by a monk who lived in the castle, the only time you could marvel at Ralph quite happily sitting there, quietly absorbed in reading. Ralph loved his lessons. He was a very inquisitive boy, itching with curiosity, and he relished how reading made him think and ask questions. He especially enjoyed chatting in the different languages he was taught – English, French and Latin. In spite of being enthusiastic about his lessons, Ralph knew he wasn't the best at sitting still. He found quiet concentration a bit tricky and he wasn't all that quick to pick things up – at least, not like he did when he got to be active.

Luckily, Ralph took lessons with his sister Emma and she was always on hand to help him. Emma was a good few years younger than Ralph. He always said she was half his age and twice as clever. In fact, Emma was quite the cleverest person that Ralph had ever met. When Ralph and Emma played at being knights, Emma would use her wits as much as her wooden sword to outsmart her way to victory. When Ralph was trying to grasp how to ask for food in French, Emma could fluently order an entire menu of French cuisine. When Ralph was struggling to remember Latin sentences and slowly writing them out, Emma had penned a poem and scribed a song.

Ralph's favourite creative item that Emma ever made was a picture which she painted on his wooden shield and gave to him for his birthday. It was a picture of the castle's symbol, a lion. You could spot the lion all over the castle, carved onto stone walls, on wooden tables and in tapestries hanging from the ceiling. The fierce lion represented strength and bravery, all things which Ralph aspired to. He played with his lion shield every day and dreamed that King Henry himself could see him. The king, Ralph imagined, would immediately know what a magnificent knight Ralph was going to be when he grew up, if only he could see him with his lion shield. More than anything else in the world, Ralph wished that he could impress King Henry – he wished and wished and wished. Now, as you all know, when you make a wish …

On the day the messenger arrived on horseback, Ralph was up on the castle battlements, pretending to be a knight with his wooden sword. The battlements were way up high, high enough to make your head spin, your stomach turn and your toes tingle, but oh, what fun to be up, up, up in the sky. Ralph loved to be on the battlements, surrounded by whipping air, with the green fields of Norwich stretched out for miles in front of him. He felt as though he were king of the clouds. He knew the castle was very famous for its white stones which gave the building a glowing appearance, like a huge stone beacon which could be seen from many miles away.

Ralph had his wooden sword with him and was ready as anything for an adventure. Up galloped the messenger and Ralph heard him shout, 'Make ready for the King!'

'This is it!' gasped Ralph. 'My big chance, my chance to impress King Henry!' Ralph was wildly excited, but at the same time, oddly nervous. It was rather a daunting thought, meeting a real-life hero, someone he had heard stories about and looked up to, aspired to be like. What if the king didn't like him, or just ignored him?

This was all too much, and for the first time in his life Ralph the Ready felt … well … not ready. He decided to make a plan, a plan to impress the king. An idea sprang to mind that he could put on a show, a show to show off his skills, a real showstopper of a show. This would be no easy feat, pondered Ralph, he would have to work very hard on this show. This required much thought, effort and attention to detail. If the slightest thing went wrong he could end up looking very silly.

Ralph fastened his wooden sword to his side and wandered down from the battlements. On his way, he bumped into Emma. Emma was gazing intently down at the ground as she walked. Ralph supposed she must have been deep in clever thoughts. 'What are you doing, Emma?' asked Ralph.

'Following,' said Emma.

'Following what?' asked Ralph.

Emma pointed to the floor and Ralph saw a long, sloppy, smudgy trail of big, muddy paw prints splattered in front of them like a painter had flicked a mucky brush and made a great mess. The two followed the long trail of scattered paw prints all the way down to the castle's basement. The basement was an enormous space used for storing barrels – you couldn't see the walls for all the barrels stacked on top of each other. The paw print trail was smudged all the way up a lone barrel and there, sitting on the top with a look of contented self-importance, happily oblivious to the mess he had made, was the castle cat, Smudge.

If the castle symbol was that of a fierce lion, strong and brave, Smudge was the opposite of this. He was rather a cowardly cat, who scuffled off at the merest sign of danger. Not one to exert himself, Smudge was big and round, the roundest cat you ever did see, with a round belly, a round face, round eyes and a round pink nose. He was tremendously fluffy with white and ginger patches of fur all about his terrifically round body. Smudge's job in the castle was to catch mice, although he never did. In fact, it's safe to say that Smudge never bothered to do anything that didn't involve sleeping, snacking or leaving smudgy paw prints in places he had no business to be. Catching mice just didn't make it to Smudge's 'to-do' list.

Today was no different. There sat Smudge, lazy as you like. Emma scooped up Smudge in a big cuddle in her arms and his fluffy face wrinkled with a mixture of joy and confusion. Smudge was very happy to be picked up and cuddled, although he was never sure what he did to deserve it. Nothing, as far as Ralph was concerned, although he adored Smudge all the same.

'Shall we play?' asked Emma.

'No time,' said Ralph. He wanted to play, but the thought of King Henry's arrival was pressing on his mind. 'I've got to work very hard on my show, a show to impress King Henry.'

'We'll help!' cried Emma, excited. 'At least,' she added, 'I'll help, Smudge can watch.'

Ralph gave this some thought. Smudge had an ability to look pleasantly surprised at everything, which would make him a good audience member. As for Emma, Ralph figured that two heads were better than one, and with his adventurous spirit and her brilliant cleverness they would surely come up with a fantastic show. But this most welcome offer of help somehow seemed too good to be true, too easy.

'No, I can't let you help me,' said Ralph. 'Our castle symbol is the lion, remember, to represent strength and bravery. I can't very well show King Henry how strong and brave I am if I allow my little sister and our cat to help me. This is something I must do alone.'

'Alright then,' sighed Emma. 'If that's how you feel. But you don't have to be alone, Ralph, we're always here, and asking for help wouldn't make you any less strong or brave. Everyone needs a helping hand, you know. Still, I'll leave you to practise your show.'

She wandered outside the basement with Smudge looking very comfortable in her arms.

Ralph watched them leave, his heart heavy. He did want Emma to stay – he would have been so grateful for her, no doubt, excellent help. But no, the decision was made. 'I need no help,' Ralph told himself. 'I am Ralph the Ready!' He drew his wooden sword from his side and thrust it in the air, 'Ready for adventure!'

For an entire day, Ralph worked non-stop on his show to impress King Henry. First, he worked on his swordsmanship. Ralph had his very own chainmail shirt and shiny helmet which he wore in his fighting lessons. With his wooden sword and lion shield, he figured out a performance that he could deliver alone. Into this performance, Ralph worked all his best, most fearsome moves, lunging like he meant business, swishing and swiping his sword in the air with expert speed and precision. 'The moves of an absolute champion, if I say so myself,' Ralph said so himself, to himself.

Secondly, Ralph decided to make a picture of a lion. He really wanted King Henry to be as enamoured as he was of the castle's famous symbol and, what's more, have a keepsake from his time at the castle. Ralph knew he didn't have much of an artistic eye, but he was good at making things, so he decided to carve the lion in a slab of stone.

Ralph found a good sturdy slab of stone and chiselled away for several hours. He was very pleased with the result, as his lion looked decisively fierce and bold. The carving would make an excellent keepsake for the king and he would surely be impressed with Ralph's dedication in making it.

Finally, Ralph decided to make a pie for King Henry. He had heard all about the king's sensationally hearty appetite and vigour for devouring food. This would not be any old pie, but the best pie the king had ever tasted. The best and, most importantly, the biggest – a pie of gargantuan size, a pie to end all pies. At the sight of this pie, other pies would fall silent in awe. Ralph explained all this to the friendly cook in the castle kitchen, who listened with amusement and intrigue and then followed Ralph's instructions. The result was a pie as big as Ralph!

Ralph wanted to present the pie to King Henry, so he had to practise lifting it. It was a real balancing act to walk without wobbling over and the cook suggested he should have some help, but Ralph was adamant he could manage alone. To finish off their masterful work, Ralph showed the cook how to write 'King Henry' and together they baked the letters onto the pie crust.

At last, everything was ready. Ralph had prepared a fighting performance, a marvellous lion carving and an enormous pie. King Henry could not possibly fail to be impressed. Ralph felt very happy with all his hard work and couldn't believe that he had even considered getting Emma to help him when he so clearly needed no help at all.

It was the day of King Henry's arrival. Hundreds of people came to the castle, all dressed in very fine clothes. The women wore fancy dresses which flowed to the ground. Everyone wanted to look their best for King Henry. There was much chattering and excitement, a real buzz in the air. Everyone gathered in the banquet hall where a great feast had been prepared. The banquet hall was an enormous room, large and vast enough to house a family of giants. The room was decorated beautifully with bright banners of red, blue and gold, and many of the banners that hung elegantly from the ceiling had pictures of lions on them. The lions looked so fierce and proud that you could almost hear them roar.

In the middle of the room stood a table so long that, if it was a river, you could glide across on a boat at breakfast and reach the other side round about teatime. The table was covered with food – fruit, vegetables, honey and pies, lots of pies. Under this table, hid Ralph. Ralph was the most ready he had ever been, fully prepared in his chainmail shirt and shiny helmet complete with his wooden sword and lion shield. He had practised his fighting performance all night and just couldn't wait to show everyone. Beside him was the stone carving of the lion which Ralph would present to King Henry after his performance. As for the pie, Ralph had arranged that, on his signal, the cook would bring the pie to the banquet hall entrance and Ralph would take it from there. All his hard work was about to be complete and he could scarcely contain his excitement.

Ralph couldn't see the room from under the table, only people's feet, so he was unsure of how he would spot King Henry, but Ralph didn't need to worry about this because the king's arrival was about to become very clear. All of a sudden, the room fell silent. Ralph held his breath. From a distance, he heard the sound of sturdy, decisive footsteps slapping across the stone floor. Then Ralph heard the rather shrill voice of a man announce, 'His Royal Highness, King Henry!'

Ralph could feel the sense of excitement as it hovered intensely in the air. What was the most important man in all the land about to say to the people of Norwich Castle? Probably, thought Ralph, the most important thing that he had ever heard.

'Bonjour!' came a booming, boisterous and rather jolly voice. 'I'm hungry. Let's eat!'

Well, it wasn't exactly the most important thing that Ralph had ever heard but it certainly hit the right note because the response was a thunderous round of applause followed by much chomping, chewing, chatting and laughter. Now was the time, thought Ralph, while everyone was happy and in high spirits, the perfect time to introduce some invigorating entertainment – his fighting show. Ralph clutched his wooden sword in one hand, his lion shield in the other hand and with all the courage he could muster, shot out from under the table.

'Ralph the Ready, ready for adventure!'

The room suddenly fell silent in surprise. Now boldly standing on his own two feet, Ralph saw the bemused faces of the many people in front of him as they watched, still as statues, some holding goblets in mid-air, some with pies hanging at their open jaws. At the middle of the table on a grand chair sat the man behind the boisterous voice, King Henry. He was a young man, hale and hearty. There was an air of triumph about him. This was a man used to victories, and who anticipated winning many more. He was exceptionally strong, with broad shoulders, and his face was pleasant with piercing eyes, assured features, a strong jaw and round cheeks, currently rosy from cheerfully tucking into food. If ever a person resembled our symbol of the lion, thought Ralph, that person is King Henry.

Next to King Henry sat a small man who, in contrast, reminded Ralph of a little weasel. It was something in the tense, cunning slant of his features that made Ralph think of a weasel. The man had a pinched face, pointy nose and flimsy grey hair. Ralph assumed this was the man with the shrill voice who had introduced the king. He looked back at King Henry and saw a distinct look of confusion wrinkle the king's brow, he clearly wasn't sure what to make of all this. Neither, for that matter, was Ralph.

Seeing everyone in front of him like that, Ralph suddenly felt so nervous that he forgot what he was about to do. 'Quick, Ralph, quick, do something now!' his head urged him, 'You can't just leave King Henry sitting there confused, he won't be impressed at all.' Ralph shook away his nerves as best he could and began his fighting performance. But those nerves were pesky things. Ralph found that his hands were trembling, he couldn't hold his wooden sword properly and his lion shield was wobbling about. What's more, he kept forgetting all the moves and his feet danced around desperately as he tried to remember. All the while, Ralph gazed at King Henry's face, which was a picture of bewilderment. This was not the reaction Ralph was hoping for at all. The king was far from impressed. The next thing Ralph knew he had tripped over his own feet and tumbled down flat on the ground where he lay in a heap of embarrassment.

'What is this preposterous display?' piped up the little weasel man. 'Don't you realise, boy, that this is the king? Do not make a fool of yourself in front of …'

But before he could finish he was interrupted by a girl, who stood up suddenly. It was Emma. Bold as can be, she began to laugh out loud. 'That's hilarious, Ralph,' she cried. 'How funny!'

'Thanks a bunch, Emma,' Ralph mumbled under his breath, 'You've just made it even worse!'

But as Emma kept laughing, Ralph suddenly realised what his clever sister was doing.

'He's practised ever so hard,' she told everyone around her. 'He's a real natural at comedy. Did you see that perfect comedic timing as he tumbled to the floor?'

This remark was followed by many teeters of laughter. The teeters grew louder and louder until the entire banquet hall was in a great, laughing uproar. Ralph gaped at King Henry, who burst into brazen, roaring laughter. '*Excellent, c'est magnifique!*' he boomed. 'Some quality entertainment. I love to laugh!' He turned to the little weasel man at his side, 'Now don't be such a bore, Sir Egglebert! This young Ralph has clearly worked very hard to be so silly. Lighten up and laugh!' He called out to Ralph, 'Bravo, talented young fellow, do the falling over bit again!'

Ralph got up, then promptly fell down again. The room was in absolute stitches and people cried out, 'Again! Again!'. Heartened by his adoring fans, Ralph began to enjoy himself and put on a really good comedy show where he fought very badly and fell on the floor. Everyone laughed and laughed and laughed, and King Henry laughed loudest and hardest of all, clutching his sides, tears streaming down his rosy cheeks, 'Ahahahahah! Ahahahahah! Ahahahahah! Wonderful showmanship! What a talent! The boy's a natural!'

In the midst of his performance, Ralph found time to focus on Emma in the crowd and mouth, 'Thank you!' Then, at the height of his success, Ralph decided that it would be a great time to go and get his present for King Henry. He quickly dodged under the table and emerged seconds later with his lion carving.

'Your Highness,' Ralph announced, 'I made this for you because you are this lion.' He thrust the carving in front of him for all to see, feeling sure that King Henry would be delighted that he had compared him to such a fierce, brave, strong lion. Ralph's expectations, however, were shattered as his enraptured audience suddenly fell into stark, cold silence. All eyes were fixated on him with horror. King Henry, once again, wrinkled his brow in confusion.

Sir Egglebert broke the awkward silence. 'What is this insult?' he asked sharply.

'Insult?' Ralph repeated, a feeling of terror in his stomach.

'Yes,' said Sir Egglebert, 'insult. What, precisely, do you mean when you say that King Henry is that lion? Are you saying that our noble king is a mess?'

Now it was Ralph's turn to wrinkle his brow in confusion. Slowly, he looked down at the carving in his hands. Oh Smudge! Oh no! That silly cat must have been for a walk under the table because he had left big fat smudgy paw prints all over the carving and Ralph hadn't noticed them in his haste to grab it. You could hardly see the lion through the many paw prints. Ralph's heart skipped a beat as he realised he had just compared King Henry to a disaster. How was he going to get out of this?

It was clever Emma to the rescue again. Calmly, she stood up and said, 'Remarkable. Yes, yes, it does remind me of our heroic King.

Ralph has boldly expressed the courage and triumph of King Henry through this carving. There sits the mighty lion and each paw print represents all the castles of his kingdom. Just look at all those castles!'

Slowly, King Henry's furrowed brow began to smooth and a smile spread across his face. 'Oh, I see, so I'm the lion and every paw print represents the castles of my kingdom … *c'est fantastique, j'adore*, I love it!'

Ralph was ecstatic to hear those words from King Henry, and Emma was clearly enjoying herself now; 'You know, the sense of theatre in the carving makes me want to roar like a lion.'

'Oh bravo, brilliant idea!' cried the king. 'Come on everyone, let's all roar like lions.'

Everyone roared like lions and the king roared loudest and hardest of all, each mighty roar accompanied by a fist punch to the air, 'Roooarrrrr! Rooooarrrr! Rooooooooaaaarrr!'

In all the commotion Ralph nodded a big 'thank you' to Emma.

'*Excellent, excellent*, that was enormously enjoyable!' beamed King Henry. 'Now, let us return to this ravishing feast.' Everyone merrily began to eat again.

This, thought Ralph, was the perfect opportunity for the pie. He could see the cook had arrived with the gigantic pie at the entrance to the banquet hall. Ralph quickly sneaked off to take the pie from him. Ralph balanced the enormous pie on his hands and began to stride towards King Henry in his grand seat, although, from behind the pie, he couldn't really see where he was going, he wibbled and wobbled this way and that. 'Your Highness,' he announced from behind the pie, 'I made this pie especially for ...'

All of a sudden, Smudge dashed out from under the table and ran in front of Ralph. It was the one moment of the one day in Smudge's entire life that, quite without warning and for reasons unknown, he decided to do his job and chase a mouse. It was the worst possible moment of the worst possible day that Smudge could have chosen to do this. Ralph stumbled over Smudge's swishing tail. The next thing he knew, he had tripped, tippled, toppled, tumbled and … oh no … oh no … splat! The pie sprang from his hands, sailed through the air and landed straight on King Henry's face!

'… you,' Ralph whimpered the end of his sentence, a tiny squeak of a whimper.

King Henry didn't move a muscle. Crumbles of pie crust fell from his face to his shoulders, and still he moved not a jot. He must be fuming with anger under there, thought Ralph, not that he could tell, as the king's face was completely covered with splattered pie. Sir Egglebert rose furiously from his seat. 'This time, boy, you really have taken things too far!' His voice was sharp as glass. 'I suppose you think this is all a game, eh? Just a bit of fun. Well, look where your fun has got you.'

Ralph looked round at the room of horrified faces. Everyone was aghast at what had just happened. Sir Egglebert raised his hand towards King Henry. 'Behold, the pie-covered King!'

Ralph was in for it now and he knew it. There was no coming back from the trouble he was in. His time was up, his days were numbered, he was done for. Desperately Ralph gaped at Emma. Surely his clever sister would think of something. But Emma only blinked back in despair. What could she do?

'Oh, please think of something Emma,' Ralph willed her helplessly from under his breath. 'Please, my clever, wonderful sister, help me, please, please, please …'

Emma's lips quivered as though an idea was on the tip of her tongue, then all of a sudden, her mouth flung open and she yelled, 'Pie fight!' Ralph stared at his sister in awe. The next thing he knew, she was charging towards him armed with a pie which she threw in his face. Splat!

'Pie fight! Hooray!' Ralph cried. He snatched a pie from the table and threw it in Emma's face.

'*Excellent, excellent*, good sport!' Ralph heard King Henry cry. 'I love a pie fight!' The king picked up a pie and hurled it towards Sir Egglebert. 'Here Sir Egglebert, take that!' Splat! The pie landed straight in Sir Egglebert's face. To Ralph's surprise, he could have sworn he saw Sir Egglebert's stern face break into a smile from beneath all that pie and his shoulders shook with laughter.

'Good shot, Your Highness. Well done!'

There was a great excited scramble as everyone began grabbing pies and hurtling them at each other with glee. Splat! Splat! Splat! The glorious pie fight continued in full swing until at last everyone was so exhausted with laughter and pie throwing they all had to stop.

'I have had the most fantastically fun day,' declared King Henry. He raised his goblet. 'Let us all drink to young Ralph here, who made this happen. What was it I heard you call yourself earlier, boy? Ralph the …'

'Ralph the Ready, Your Highness,' Ralph told him.

'Well, Ralph the Ready,' said King Henry, 'first you are a hilarious entertainer, then a talented artist and now a fantastic pie fighter. I am mightily impressed.'

These were the words Ralph had longed to hear, but it didn't feel right for only him alone to hear them. 'Thank you, Your Highness,' he said. 'But please, let's not just drink to me. You see, this was all down to my clever sister, Emma. She's the cleverest person in all the world and I was only able to do this because of her. Everything I did was her idea. She helped me.'

'*Excellent, très bien!*' beamed King Henry. 'I'm never one to turn down an offer of help. I always say two heads are better than one. Let us drink to the both of you.' He launched his goblet high in the air. 'To Ralph the Ready and Emma the Clever. I am mightily impressed with both of you. Thank you for this great adventure!'

And so, you see, Ralph the Ready did need his sister's help after all and, what's more, he was glad to have it. The two continued to help each other always, even when they had grown up and flown the nest, although they had many more adventures to share before that happened.

That's the end of the story, but it doesn't have to end there for you, because if you visit Norwich

Castle, you are sure to have a great adventure! But, for now, it's goodbye from Ralph the Ready, Emma the Clever and Smudge the cat who, in his own special, smudgy way, had helped out that day and got lots of cuddles.

2

THE STORY WEAVERS

INSPIRED BY STRANGERS' HALL

*In the Story – The Great Hall,
the Great Chamber, a Baltic Oak Closet
and the Little Bed Chamber*

*O*nce upon a time, hundreds of years ago, there lived a girl who loved to make up stories. The girl's name was Martha, as lively and bright a girl as ever you could meet, and be sure that if you did meet her, she would straight away tell you a story. She could tell you the real story of how she lived in a house with her mother and father, who worked as grocers in Norfolk during the reign of Queen Elizabeth the First. The queen, Martha would tell you, was a remarkable woman, brave and kind, with hair as red as the royal jewels in her crown.

But she could just as well tell you all sorts of made-up stories, fresh from her wild imagination, stories about the mischievous faery who lived under her bed and would grant you wishes if you brought her honey, only to give you the opposite of what you wished for. Then there was the goose in their garden, who laid eggs of solid gold unless you asked it to, then it would just lay normal eggs. Not to mention the winter dragon with scales of ice, who hid in shady corners of their garden and sulkily breathed frost over the flowers until the arrival of the spring dragon with scales as green as grass, who would breathe life back into all that surrounded him. When he spread his wings the flowers burst into bloom.

Sometimes, Martha had fun mixing what was real with what was made up. She would imagine stories where the very real Queen Elizabeth the First met the very made-up winter dragon and rode on his back. Elegant and magnificent, the queen soared through the silver clouds, her red hair flying behind her like a crimson whirlwind in the sky.

Stories about this, stories about that, stories about happy vagabonds, fearsome ogres, singing swans, curious cats, stories about him, her, both of them and you … if only she had someone to tell them to! You see, Martha didn't have any brothers or sisters. Her parents were always busy with one thing or the other, and she spent a good deal of time alone. Being alone was nice sometimes – she enjoyed quiet time – but she also liked to make a noise, run around, laugh and play, and this was not so enjoyable to do on her own. Martha would have loved to have a friend she could talk to, play with and, best of all, share her stories with. It seemed to her that she would always be a storyteller with no one to tell stories to forever more.

But that is not how this story goes.

One day, Martha's mother announced to her, clear out of the blue, that they were going to stay with her Aunt Elizabeth and Uncle Thomas in their lovely house in Norwich. Mother explained that she and Father hadn't seen that side of the family for a while and it would be nice to spend some time with them. Martha felt very excited about going somewhere different and meeting new people. A chance for her to make friends! She liked the sound of staying in a lovely house and immediately started to make up stories about it in her head.

When she arrived at the house, however, she soon discovered that it was even more lovely than she had imagined. Aunt Elizabeth and Uncle Thomas were there to greet the family on their arrival and welcomed them into the Great Hall. The Great Hall was an enormous room, so big that when they spoke, their voices bounced off the walls, and the ceiling was so high that just to peer up at it made Martha feel giddy. Looking around her, Martha saw that everything inside the room was impressive. There was a beautiful bay window which let in floods of light, an elaborately carved table and chairs and, to the right of the room, a grand staircase which led up onto a balcony. Just to set foot on that grand staircase made Martha feel as though she were terribly important.

Uncle Thomas led them up the stairs until they reached the balcony, then told her to look out of a small window which overlooked the garden. The garden was a delightful sight, with lots of flowers, and at the end of the lawn was a church which her uncle told her was St Gregory's Church. Then, he took them on a tour of the house which was a maze of many rooms and corridors.

In particular, Martha liked the Great Chamber in the west wing. The room consisted of wooden floors and walls with a large closet built into the wall. It was very dark oak, and Uncle Thomas told her that it was Baltic oak, which made it very special. There was a large fireplace at the end of the room and Martha thought it would be nice to curl up in front of that fireplace with a blanket and tell stories. What with it being so dark, decorative and warm, the room had rather a mysterious atmosphere and Martha felt a strange but exciting feeling, as though something wonderful was going to happen.

At the end of the tour, Martha was taken to the little bed chamber where she was to sleep at night. She was relieved to find the room lived up to its name in being 'little', as she would have felt rather nervous sleeping in a room as big and grand as the Great Hall. Martha had so many stories bubbling around inside her head inspired by the house, she thought the little bed chamber seemed a nice, peaceful spot to sit and think about them. And she certainly had time for thinking. Once again, Martha found that, more often than not, she was alone, as the grown-ups were always talking together.

'I suppose I'll just tell stories to no one but myself, forever and ever,' thought Martha.

But that is not how this story goes.

One afternoon, Martha was sitting on her bed telling herself the story of the nosy neighbour whose nose grew bigger the nosier he got, when suddenly, she heard lots of noises coming from downstairs like hundreds of people chattering and clattering about, and so, much like her character in the story, she decided to go and have a nose around. There were lots of people in the Great Hall. Where had they come from? What were they doing there? Martha hurried down the grand staircase to talk to them and, at the bottom, bumped into Uncle Thomas.

'Who are all these people?' she asked him.

'They are the strangers,' Uncle Thomas told her.

'Strangers?' Martha repeated, confused. 'If they are strangers, why are they in the house?'

'Because I invited them,' Uncle Thomas smiled. 'These strangers are very talented weavers. I invited them to help us grow our cloth industry in Norwich. I got permission to invite them from none other than Queen Elizabeth herself.'

Martha gasped. If Queen Elizabeth said that the strangers could come, then they must be very important people. 'Where have they come from?' she asked.

'From countries overseas,' said Uncle Thomas, 'Holland, Belgium and Luxembourg. They are going to stay here with us while they weave. I thought they could stay in the Great Chamber.'

'Well,' said Martha, 'if they are going to stay then they won't be strangers for long.'

For the rest of the day, the house was filled with the hustle and bustle of the strangers' arrival. They were very vibrant people and Martha enjoyed hearing snippets of their different languages as they chatted and sang songs. She felt swept up in the liveliness of it all and was eager to make friends with them. 'Hello, my name's Martha. You must have had a long journey. Would you like to hear a story?'

But they were just so busy talking to each other and getting used to their new surroundings that nobody noticed her. She decided that she would go back to her room and make up lots of new stories for these strangers to listen to, so that when things had calmed down a bit she would be ready for her new audience. That night, Martha couldn't sleep for all the stories buzzing in her head, stories for the strangers. It was a very dark night, but Martha had a small candle in a candlestick by her bed and as the flame flickered, she watched it cast playful shadows against the wall. She noticed that if she lifted her hand she could make shadow patterns on the wall by moving her fingers. Outside, the wind was howling; it rattled the windows and whirled through the corridors, whoosh! Martha heard the wind, whoosh! whoosh!

And then she heard something else. It sounded as if someone was crying. Martha didn't like to hear the sound of someone being upset and wanted to see what the matter was and whether she could help. It did seem a bit of a bother to get out of bed on a cold and blustery night, after all, the crying might only be the sound of the wind, she could just roll over in bed …

But that is not how this story goes.

Martha slipped out of bed, took the candlestick to light her way and tiptoed out of her room, through the corridors of the house, following the sound of the crying. At last, she found herself approaching the Great Chamber in the west wing. Outside the door of the Great Chamber, a girl was sitting on the floor sobbing, arms wrapped around herself, her figure shrouded by her long ebony hair. Martha realised the girl must have been one of the strangers, as she knew they were sleeping inside the Great Chamber. The girl had clearly gone outside the room to cry alone, so Martha hoped she didn't mind her turning up.

'Hello,' Martha whispered softly, because she didn't want to startle the girl. 'Why are you crying?'

The girl looked up, her face wet with tears. She looked a little surprised to see a figure with a candle coming towards her. Martha gave her a big warm smile to show that she was friendly and was pleased to see the girl smile back. 'My name is Martha,' said Martha. 'What's your name?'

The girl said nothing, but sniffed, although she was still smiling. She seemed glad to have company.

'You must be one of the strangers.' Martha edged a little closer to the girl. 'It must be quite frightening to be somewhere completely different and feel like you are far away from home. But you're not alone here. Not at all. I would like for us to be friends.'

She wondered what she could do to cheer the girl up. 'I'm very good at telling stories. I could tell you a story now, if you like.'

Still the girl said nothing. But, of course, Martha realised, if she was from another country then perhaps she couldn't speak English. If the girl came from Holland, Belgium or Luxembourg then her language must be Dutch or Flemish. How could she tell a story when the girl wouldn't understand what she was saying? She would have to act it out. Martha quickly thought of a story that just might work as a performance; the story of the mouse who outran a lion.

'Once upon a time there lived a clever little mouse ...' She nuzzled up her face, twitched her nose like a mouse and gave a 'squeak!' It was an amusing tale; one day a mouse came across a lion and challenged him to a competition in which he would prove he was just as big as the lion was. The lion laughed at such nonsense; a tiny mouse could never be as big as him, the King of Beasts. But the pesky mouse outwitted the silly lion with tricks and words. He made a fool of the lion and proved he was bigger than him in more ways than one. Martha made roaring noises when she played the lion and pulled the funny faces he made when he was confused and defeated. Sometimes, she held up the candle against the wall and cast shadow patterns with her hands. If she rolled up the fist of her right hand into a little ball and stuck the two fingers of her left hand behind it for ears, it looked like the mouse, running along the wall.

The girl was smiling and giggling the whole time. When Martha finished telling the story, the girl clapped her hands.

'I suppose you should probably get some sleep now inside the Great Chamber, with your family and friends,' said Martha. 'And I think I'd best get to bed too. I do hope you feel a bit better. Let's meet again tomorrow and I'll tell you another story.'

She had just got up and was about to leave when she felt a tug at her nightdress. She turned around and saw the girl point to herself, 'Beatrix.'

Martha nodded and smiled. 'I'll see you tomorrow, Beatrix.'

The next day, Martha returned to the Great Chamber to see that the strangers had started to do their weaving. They had set up looms, which were large wooden objects that held the threads in place, ready to be woven. Beatrix was very happy to see Martha. She ran towards her and gave her a great big hug. If Beatrix had been shy when Martha first met her, that certainly wasn't the case anymore.

Full of energy and larger than life, Beatrix practically bounced off the walls in her eagerness to spend time with Martha. Over the next few weeks, Martha spent many happy hours with Beatrix and the strangers, although, of course, they were not strangers any more. Martha discovered that Beatrix's language was Flemish. As for the fact they couldn't understand each other, this made them wonderfully imaginative in the way they shared their time.

Martha chose very active stories which she could perform for Beatrix to watch. There was the story of the fish who swam so fast that not even the waves could keep up with him – it was said that he swam every ocean and saw the world three times over until, in the end, he made his home in a seashell. To this day, anyone who picks up that seashell and presses it to their ear can hear the fish tell tales of the things he's seen. There was the story of the princess who wore out all her shoes from dancing and there weren't enough shoemakers in the kingdom to make enough shoes to replace the ones she wore out until, in the end, it became custom for the whole kingdom to walk barefoot, just like their dancing princess. Finally, there was the story of the sly fox who tried to catch a hedgehog for breakfast until, in the end, the hedgehog tricked him into eating a prickly pine cone instead.

Martha flapped and bubbled like a fish, twirled, twizzled and swirled like a dancing princess, prowled like a fox, curled herself up into a ball and rolled like a hedgehog. Beatrix would watch mesmerised and sometimes liked to join in. When Martha told her the story of the winter and spring dragons, Beatrix insisted they go outside and pretend they were the two dragons. She liked to be the spring dragon and would spread out her arms like wings, imagining that the flowers were bursting into bloom all around her.

When they weren't storytelling and playing, Beatrix was very busy with weaving. She taught Martha how to weave; two sets of threads were woven together to make a cloth. The loom held the first set of threads in place, called warp threads, while the second threads, called the weft threads, were interlaced through them. Martha was not a natural at weaving and often muddled up the threads, which usually sparked fits of giggles for the both of them.

Over their time together, the two picked up plenty of each other's languages. Beatrix was quick to learn and once she was comfortable speaking English, the two made up a song together.

Weave me a story, weave me a song
Weave me a dream over ten foot long
Weave me a wish about to come true
Where stories are woven, I am with you.

Martha had never felt so happy. It was wonderful to have a friend and she hoped those days would go on and on.

But that is not how this story goes.

Martha's mother told her that it was time to go back to their house. 'It's time to say goodbye to the stranger now.'

'She's not a stranger,' Martha told her. 'She's my friend.'

Before she left, Martha gave Beatrix the biggest hug in all the world. 'I'll write to you every week with a new story,' she told her.

'Oh, but I won't be able to write back,' Beatrix told her. 'I can't read or write, I've never been taught.'

'It doesn't matter,' said Martha. 'Perhaps you could get someone to read them to you, it's our only way of keeping in touch. Just promise me that you will hold on to my letters.'

'I promise,' Beatrix told her.

Martha faithfully wrote letters to Beatrix with a new story every week. Story after story, week after week. She had no idea if Beatrix was getting them, but could only trust that she was keeping her promise. After a time, she heard tell that some of the strangers had moved on from the lovely house to other parts of Norwich and she wondered if Beatrix had moved with them. Martha continued to write letters without knowing if they were being read. She supposed it would be that way forever.

But that is not how this story goes.

One summer, Martha's mother told her that they were going back to see Aunt Elizabeth and Uncle Thomas at the lovely house. Martha felt a bit nervous about this, as she half expected to find her letters there, forgotten and discarded. When they arrived back at the lovely house, Martha was pleased to find that it was much the same and the air was still riddled with that mysterious and exciting atmosphere. She was taken back to the little bed chamber where she was to sleep. As soon as she entered the room, her eyes widened and her heart skipped a beat. There, on the bed, was a beautiful piece of woven cloth. The weaving was made up of lots of different pictures – pictures of all her stories.

There was the swirling crystal blue sea full of seashells of every colour and pattern, and the fish who swam faster than the waves; there was the dancing princess prancing on the turrets of a castle; there was a forest filled with animals; the fox and the hedgehog, the mouse and the lion; there was a garden with the winter and spring dragons and a sky filled with stars, butterflies and faeries, amongst many other pictures of the stories Martha had written.

Martha noticed that in the middle of the weaving was a picture she did not recognise as one of her stories. It was a donkey pulling a cart with a farmer and a girl sitting inside it.

Martha tried to remember a story she had written about a donkey, a farmer and a girl, but nothing sprang to mind. Still, she thought, it could only have been Beatrix who had woven these stories together. So, she was getting all her letters after all!

Weave me a story, weave me a song
Weave me a dream over ten foot long,
Weave me a wish about to come true
Where stories are woven, I am with you

'Boo!'

Martha spun round. At the doorway stood Beatrix! She bounced up to Martha and gave her a hug bigger than the world.

'Oh, Beatrix, it's you!' Martha cried. 'I'm so glad you're here. I thought perhaps you had moved.'

'Some of the strangers moved, but not me!' said Beatrix. 'And some new strangers have arrived and joined us too. Though of course, we are all good friends. No one in this house stays a stranger for long. Now, do you like the weaving I made for you?'

'It's beautiful,' said Martha. 'I love it, you are so talented. And I just can't believe that you wove all my stories.'

'Of course,' said Beatrix. 'I kept all your letters, just like I promised. I got one of the strangers to read them to me every week. And because I couldn't write back, I wove this.'

'But, what's that picture in the middle?' asked Martha. 'The one of the donkey pulling the cart with the farmer and girl? I don't remember writing that.'

'Ah well,' smiled Beatrix. 'That's *my* story. You see, I couldn't very well weave all your stories but not make up my own. Would you like to hear it?'

'Yes please!' said Martha, filled with joy that Beatrix had made up a story of her own.

'I'll act it out for you,' said Beatrix, 'just like you used to perform your stories for me. Now, get comfy.'

Martha sat down on the bed, ready to listen.

Beatrix began her story. 'Once upon a time there lived a farmer, his clever daughter and their mischievous donkey ...'

3

SIR SPECKLES

INSPIRED BY ELIZABETHAN HOUSE MUSEUM

*In the Story – The Elizabethan
Dining Room, a Lavender Basket, a Posset,
a Foot Warmer and the Birthing Room*

*O*nce upon a time, long ago, there lived a dog called Speckles, who was very forgetful. Speckles had come about his name because his soft grey fur was covered with lots of little white specks, although he could never remember how many. Speckles always looked a bit sleepy, as though he had either just woken up from a nap or was thinking how nice it would be to have one, although he could never remember how many naps he took in a day. Speckles had big floppy ears which drooped loosely about his face, just hanging there, waiting to be stroked. His huge, white, fluffy moustache sprang out busily about his nose and sometimes grew so bushy it needed a brush, although he could never remember how often.

Speckles' walk was very slow, but even so, it was a steady walk because despite being a bit absent-minded he could still be self-assured when he had a sense of purpose. His nose was keen and his round, black, button eyes were alert – they needed to be, because they were always on the hunt for something: a bone he had buried in the garden, an object he was going to use to help someone, a treat he was saving for later … If only he could remember where he had put them! Oh, forgetful Speckles! It was not at all uncommon to see Speckles wandering about, sniffing and searching for whatever he was looking for: 'Now where did I put that thing?'

Speckles lived hundreds of years ago in a time called the Elizabethan Age, because Queen Elizabeth the First ruled the land. Speckles resided in a very large and beautiful house with the Cooper family. There was Mum, Dad and their two children, Benjamin and Amelia, named after their parents, who loved to play with their dogs. Speckles was one of three dogs who lived in the Cooper household, the other two being little more than puppies, called Bounder and Biscuits. Bounder and Biscuits were very lively, excitable creatures, always bouncing, pouncing and yapping. The two puppies looked very similar, both chocolate brown with wide eyes and mischievous faces, so that Speckles could never remember which one was which.

Needless to say, it was a very noisy, vibrant house in which they all lived together. Speckles loved his home and family so much that, in spite of being a very forgetful sort of dog, he did have a mind to remember the big, important things, things which he kept close to his heart.

He always remembered how much he loved his family and that they loved him too. He always remembered to watch over the children when they were playing and, even when he napped during the day, he would sleep with one eye open, just in case his help was needed. He always remembered to chase the mice that scurried about the house, only on a Tuesday, to give them a run for their money (they were skittish mice and he rather thought they enjoyed the game).

Now, we know that Speckles had a mind to remember the big, important things which had to do with being part of the family, and so it goes without saying that Speckles well remembered that a new baby was on its way. This was exciting news for all the Coopers, and Speckles delighted in the sense of joy that filled the house in the lead-up to the baby's birthing day. That day came in spring, early in the morning, when rain drops fell softly and flowers popped up playfully from the earth where they had been sleeping to say, 'Hello, world!'

Speckles was having a mid-morning nap in the dining room, a room he was excessively fond of because it was connected to food and people, when, all of a sudden, he was startled awake by two chocolate-coloured bundles of energy skipping around him with abundant glee. 'Speckles! Speckles! Wake up, it's today!'

Bounder and Biscuits could hardly contain themselves for excitement. Topsy-turvy as can be, they somersaulted over each other, flipped, flopped, spun, swirled and cartwheeled, their tiny tails swishing and flicking like blades of grass blowing in a whirly wind. Speckles yawned sleepily and stretched his legs. He well remembered what was happening that day, although he thought it would be fun to pretend he had forgotten.

'What's today?'

'The baby boy was born this morning and we're going to meet him for the first time in the birthing room at noon, today, today, today!' cried one of them, who could have been

Bounder, or might have been Biscuits, for all that Speckles could tell the two acrobats apart as they rumbled and tumbled about.

'I know, I know,' smiled Speckles. 'There are some things I *do* remember. Now listen, you two, you'll exhaust yourselves before noon if you keep dancing about like that, all chaos and cartwheels! Why don't you put all that energy to good use and see if they need any help in the kitchen?'

'The kitchen, hooray!' the puppies yapped, 'It always smells nice in there.' Then off they dashed out of the dining room door. Speckles went to the door and watched them amused, tail wagging, as they pounded down the corridor to the kitchen in a race. 'Wheeeeee! What fun!' they giggled, in a manner so silly it made Speckles half smile and half roll his eyes.

'How could they think I would forget something as big and important as the baby being born today?' Speckles chuckled to himself. He chuckled and chuckled at the notion of forgetting something like that, chuckled and chuckled.

Then, all of a sudden, he stopped.

'What's that? I have forgotten something!'

His tail hovered in the air and his floppy ears stood upright. There was something he was supposed to remember. Oh, but what was it? The thought niggled and jiggled and wiggled in his head. What was he supposed to remember? Oh yes, he recalled he had been told by one of the children to bring something to the baby, a very special thing that only he could bring. 'A very special thing that only I could bring,' pondered Speckles. 'Oh, but what? I am so very forgetful!'

Speckles decided to embark on a quest to find the very special thing that only he could bring. He hoped he would find it before noon as he couldn't imagine turning up to the birthing room without it, whatever it was. As he had been napping in the dining room and it was the place where he spent the most time, Speckles felt almost certain that the very special thing would be in that room.

The dining room was a very large room with a grand fireplace. Speckles liked to snuggle in front of the fireplace on the comfortable floor, which was covered with rushes to keep it soft and warm, and the clock on the shelf always reminded him with a gentle tick if he was sleeping too much. At the end of the large room was a tall, sturdy wooden table which, more often than not, was covered with goblets to drink from and lots of food.

Meal times were wonderfully fun in the Cooper household and they often invited guests for much eating and talking. Everyone ate with their hands from trenchers, which were large wooden plates with a round dip in the middle where they put the food, and little holes at the side of the trenchers made useful salt holders. The grown-ups sat on tall chairs around the table to eat their food, and the children ate standing up. Bounder and Biscuits put on an acrobatic show for anyone who cared to watch. As for Speckles, he would wander about underneath the table, weaving around the children's feet, snuffling expectantly to see if anyone would drop scraps. Needless to say, they nearly always did, which, on top of his meals, made Speckles a very well-fed dog.

Speckles scrambled up onto a chair, round belly and all, and sniffed his nose along the table's surface. The trenchers were clean of food, and a good thing too, or else Speckles would certainly have gobbled any morsels up. He was sure that the special thing that only he could bring to the baby wasn't a trencher, because the baby couldn't very well eat from one of those yet. All of a sudden, he smelled a very lovely, musky, sweet and potent smell, a smell which danced playfully about his nose and he slowly recognised it as the smell of lavender. There, in the middle of the table was a little basket containing some bundles of lavender. Lavender baskets were dotted about the house in various places to make everything smell nice.

'Are you the thing? The very special thing that only I could bring?'

Yes, of course, this was it! The new baby would surely like some sweet-smelling lavender. 'Yes, a basket of lavender, of course. I'll bring it this afternoon,' thought Speckles, 'and the baby will smell it and, oh, how pleased he'll be that I brought this very special thing that only I could bring, only I could bring a basket of ... only I ... only ... only.' No, wait – no, no, no! That wasn't it at all. There would already be lavender baskets in the birthing room and if there weren't, there soon would be, because that was precisely the sort of thing that *anyone* could bring. He must continue his quest.

Nonetheless, Speckles picked up the basket in his teeth and put it down on the floor against the wall. It might not be the very special thing that only he could bring, but it was still a nice idea and he decided that he would take it to the baby all the same.

The next thing to grab Speckles' attention was a small cupboard on the wall opposite the grand fireplace. Speckles snooped up to the cupboard doors which were swinging open slightly. Inside the cupboard were three shelves and he pressed his paws up to the bottom shelf to examine further. On the bottom shelf stood a rather intriguing object. It was a round sort of shiny bottle with a stopper at the top. Speckles knew that the object was called a posset and was used as a money box to put coins in. He knew this because Benjamin and Amelia would often squabble about who got to use the posset when they got their pocket money.

'Are you the thing, the very special thing that only I could bring?'

Yes, of course, it made sense, a posset, the very thing! The baby would surely need a money box to collect his coins in, as soon as he started to get his pocket money. 'Only I could bring this posset,' thought Speckles. 'Only I could, only … only no, wait, no, no, no!' What use would a posset be to a baby? The baby, he realised, wouldn't have any pocket money until he was a good few years older. Besides, the posset was the sort of thing that *anyone* could bring. 'Silly Speckles,' he scolded himself. Nonetheless, the posset was a pleasantly smooth and shiny object and Speckles supposed that the baby might like to touch it. Speckles caught the posset between his teeth and placed it carefully in the lavender basket at the side of the room. He would take both those things to the baby – he might as well.

Speckles went back to the cupboard, as usual his nose taking the lead in the inspection, sniffing along the shelves. On the second shelf up sat a rather beautiful object. It was a long, square box elaborately decorated with gold patterns. Speckles knew it was a foot warmer because he had seen the family place it under their feet from time to time on winter evenings. There was a lid on the box and something warm went inside it. Then, you could press your feet against the box and have nice, toasty warm feet.

The very idea made him feel all cosy and snug. Speckles squinted quizzically at the endearingly pretty foot warmer. 'Are you the thing? The very special thing that only I could bring?'

It did seem like a nice present but, as with the lavender basket and posset, it struck Speckles that the foot warmer was the sort of thing that *anyone* could bring. He had specifically been instructed to bring something that only he, Speckles, could bring. A very special thing. It couldn't be the foot warmer. Nonetheless, Speckles decided to add the foot warmer to his basket of goodies. If he couldn't remember what he was supposed to bring, he might as well bring lots of other nice things in the hope that this would make up for it. He sensed that he was getting warmer to remembering what it was though and, having discovered these three lovely objects, felt encouraged to keep searching on his quest.

'I'll definitely keep searching on my quest,' said Speckles. 'I'll keep searching and searching and searching … right after I've had a short nap …' He could feel his fluffy eyelids beginning to close. After all, it had already been a busy day, what with finding all those objects. 'Just five minutes,' Speckles yawned as he lay down on the rush floor and curled into a ball. 'Just five, very quick minutes.'

'Speckles! Oh, Speckles!'

Speckles' eyes darted open. A chocolate-brown puppy that could have been Bounder, or might have been Biscuits, was doing a roly-poly right up to Speckles' nose, while the other twirled abundantly around him.

'It's time, Speckles! It's noon!' they chanted.

'What?' cried Speckles, 'But I've only been asleep for five minutes. Haven't I? Haven't I?' He looked at the clock and, to his dismay, saw that it was, indeed, noon. He had overslept!

'Oh no, it can't be!' cried Speckles. 'But I've forgotten … that is to say, I've not yet remembered, or found the very special thing that only I could bring.'

'Oh Speckles,' the puppies laughed cheekily, 'you're pretending to forget again.'

'No, no,' sighed Speckles. 'This time, I really have forgotten. Oh well, I suppose it can't be helped now. I'll just have to bring the three objects I found earlier today and hope that no one minds I forgot the very special thing.'

'A very special thing! A very special thing!' the puppies sang nonsensically as they danced around Speckles.

'Stop being silly,' said Speckles. 'Now come on, let's go upstairs to the birthing room.'

Bounder and Biscuits sprang to the staircase outside the dining room. Speckles picked up the lavender basket containing the posset and foot warmer and, holding it between his teeth, followed the puppies up the staircase. Bounder and Biscuits bounced up each step with such vigour they sometimes tumbled backwards, so Speckles stayed close behind, ready to catch them in his basket if they fell back too far. Once they had all made it up the stairs, the puppies scurried and skidded towards the door of the birthing room. The door flung open as though the three dogs were expected.

Speckles poked his head round the door. The birthing room was a very large room covered with elaborate wooden panels. There, in the middle of the room stood a grand bed on which Mum was sitting with the new baby boy in her arms. He looked very bouncy and happy. Dad was standing by the bed, a huge smile on his face. Benjamin and Amelia were waiting eagerly for the dogs. They both had wooden toy swords with them and had clearly been playing their favourite game of jousting knights, perhaps to put on a show for the baby. Bounder and Biscuits ran ecstatically towards the children and jumped into their arms. As for Speckles, he crossed the threshold slowly and somewhat sheepishly, feeling rather anxious that he hadn't brought the very special thing that only he could bring. It seemed to Speckles that he had let people down and he hated to do that.

'Oh Speckles!' cried Amelia. 'What's that you've got there in your mouth?' She let one of the puppies, who might have been Bounder or could have been Biscuits, tumble from her arms onto the bed and ran up to Speckles as he hovered at the doorway. Amelia took the lavender basket with the posset and foot warmer from Speckles' mouth.

'Oh, look everyone,' she said, 'Speckles has brought all these nice things for the baby, how lovely!' She reached down and nuzzled his fur. 'Though I'm sure you didn't have to do that, you silly dog.'

'I know why he's brought them,' said Benjamin. 'It's because I told him to bring a very special thing that only he could bring. Knowing Speckles, he probably forgot what it was, so he's brought these other things instead.'

He looked Speckles in the eyes, 'Well Speckles, did you remember to bring the very special thing that only you could bring?'

Speckles looked down at his paws. He felt very ashamed, but much to his surprise, he heard Benjamin laugh. 'Of *course* you remembered,' Benjamin said. 'The very special thing that only you could bring was *you!*'

Speckles looked up, amazed. Of course – he remembered now what Benjamin had told him

– he just had to bring himself, *he* was the very special thing!

Benjamin took his wooden toy sword and placed it on Speckles' shoulder. 'I knight you Sir Speckles, a dog so forgetful he forgot how special he is. It's a good thing we're all here to remind him!'

Sir Speckles was overjoyed and, for all his forgetfulness, he was sure that this was a very big and important day he would remember forever.

4

A SKY FULL OF HERRINGS

INSPIRED BY TIME AND TIDE MUSEUM

*In the Story – A Smoke House
and a Drifter Boat*

Once upon a time, there lived a boy called Jim, who found his home in a sky full of herrings.

'A sky full of herrings?' you say, 'What nonsense! Herrings are fish, surely you mean "a sea full of herrings"!'

And what of this Jim, why should he find his home in such a peculiar place? Well, to understand the beginning of this story, you need to read on to the end, which is to say that, by the end of this story, you will understand the beginning.

In the first instance, you need to find out what manner of home Jim lived in, before he found this 'sky full of herrings'.

Jim lived in a time – oh, what a time! – hundreds of years ago, when Queen Victoria sat on the throne and many exciting things were happening and important discoveries were being made. Jim lived in a town – oh, what a town! – a town called Great Yarmouth, on the coast in Norfolk at the mouth of the River Yare, a wonderful town where you could run to the seashore and watch the fishing boats bob up and down on the waves, feel the sand between your toes and take in the fresh sea air, crisp and sharp enough to clean your boots on.

Jim lived on a street – oh, what a street! – a street lined with pretty houses painted all different colours – warm peach, dusky yellow, pink berry, sky blue – a street of cobbled paths and cats jumping across the rooftops. It was close enough to the sea that you could smell the salt in the air, feel the whip of the wind against your cheek and hear the sea gulls cry and the fisherman sing. Jim lived in a house – oh, what a … oh, what a … – oh dear, Jim's house was nothing but a dusty old, rusty old, fusty old wooden box shoved up against a wall on the street. You see, Jim was a street kid with no family, no money and no one to look after him.

However, being bright and resourceful, Jim looked after himself. He had fashioned a house for himself out of a wooden box. It was very small, so that he always had to sit down when he was inside it. The cracks in the wooden box were the windows and he had made a round hole at the bottom for a door; a door he had to crawl through! Not without a touch of imagination, Jim had even placed a smaller box on top of his house to look like a chimney. After all, thought Jim, a house can be made from anything, from shoes or sticks or bits of string. If it has walls and a ceiling, it's still a house.

But a home, now that was a different matter. A home, thought Jim, is a place where you are surrounded by people who care about you. It doesn't matter where in the world this home is, how big or small, as long as the people who care about you are there.

Jim was surrounded by the people who lived in the neighbouring houses on the street. They didn't seem to mind him living in a wooden box on their street, they never asked him to leave, and sometimes they would bring him scraps of their leftover food or blankets when it was cold. But Jim knew that they were just putting up with him really, it wasn't the same. At night alone, curled up in his wooden box, he felt very lonely indeed. He would snuggle up in his blanket and dream of being surrounded by people who cared about him and whom he cared about too. With a heavy heart, Jim knew that his house was not a home.

And so, now you've found out what manner of home Jim lived in before he found the 'sky full of herrings'. Not a home at all. Just a house that wasn't a home.

One morning, Jim woke up in his house that wasn't a home to find that rain was pelting down, hard and fast through the cracks of the wooden box. Jim was used to bad weather, but this rain was particularly nasty and wouldn't stop, no matter how much he asked it to. In no time at all, he was wet through and through, cold and shivering.

'Very well,' thought Jim, 'if this rain won't quit then neither will I!' He went outside and did what he would always do on any given day – jumping and whistling. Jim could jump as high as any cat that sprang across the rooftops. He jumped so high to impress passers-by that they threw coins at him. Jim's whistle was loud and clear and he could whistle any song you asked him to, though he liked the jolly songs best. All day, every day, Jim jumped and whistled, jumped and whistled, and people would throw money at him so that he could go and buy food.

Today was no exception. It was a bit slippery for jumping, what with all the puddles on the ground, but he could still whistle and he did just that; it was the happiest, cheeriest, brightest whistle he could whistle. That rain wasn't going to dampen his spirits or stop him, he decided.

'Used to rain, are you, lad?'

A voice from nowhere startled Jim. He saw that a man was standing next to him, watching him with interest. The man was smiling; he looked friendly and was dressed in an oil skin sou'wester and boots so that Jim could tell he was a fisherman.

'I'm used to rain, right enough,' Jim told the fisherman. 'It doesn't bother me, not a jot, oh no it doesn't.'

'Well,' said the fisherman, 'that's good to hear. We're looking for young men to come and work as fishermen. As long as you don't mind hard work, getting wet, hard work, getting wet and more hard work, then you might have what it takes. You just never know what type of weather we might have when we sail out in our boats off the coast. Sometimes a storm with the rain coming down, down, down. You've got to be made of tough stuff, steeled against it. But if you're used to working in the rain then you may well have good sea legs.'

Jim looked down at his legs. 'Look like normal legs to me.'

'No, lad,' laughed the fisherman. 'Sea legs, meaning that you could cope with sailing the sea; all wind and weathers, you're seasoned to it. Now, do you think you would like a job as a fisherman?'

'Me, a fisherman?' said Jim. He had never been in a boat before and wasn't sure how he would feel about it, but nonetheless, he was very eager to have a job and make his way in the world. 'That means I could earn a living.'

'That's right, lad,' said the fisherman. 'One day, you might even be able to afford a roof over your head, a bit bigger and better than that wooden box which appears to be your home.'

'House,' Jim corrected him. 'It's my house that isn't a home. Yes, I would like a job as a fisherman.'

'Very well,' the fishermen said. 'First of all, let's find out if you have what it takes. We'll have a trial run to see if you're up to the job and, if it goes well, you can be a fisherman and earn a living. Later today, come and join us at the port to catch herrings. Arrive when it's dark. We fish throughout the night until it's so early that not even the early birds have had their breakfast. Ask for Charlie, that's me. I'll see you there.'

'See you there, Charlie,' said Jim. He felt very excited; this was a big chance. Tomorrow, he would have to work very hard to prove himself to Charlie and the other fishermen, but once that was done, he would have a job, a real job. The trial run had to go well, it just had to.

Later that day, just as it grew dark, Jim arrived at the port. He had hoped that the weather would calm down a bit after he met Charlie but no such luck. If anything, it had got worse. The rain was coming down in bucket loads. Jim saw that by the seashore were gathered ten fishermen loading nets onto a boat. The boat was very big and looked rather grand and elegant, painted red, white and blue with a tall mast in the middle, and the sail was a big flappy thing blowing about in the wind.

'This here boat is called a drifter,' Charlie explained to him, once Jim had caught up with the fishermen. 'You see, herrings swim close to the surface of the water, so we fishermen skim the nets across the top of the water and the herrings swim in. We leave the nets to drift on the water for a very long time. That's why this type of fishing is known as drift netting and the boat, a drifter. Now, come along, climb on board, lad, it's time to set sail.'

Jim clambered on board the boat, the first time he had ever set foot on a boat in his life. It felt strange not to be on dry land any more. His feet were bobbing up and down beneath him to the rhythm of the waves, up and down, up and down. 'Oo-er,' thought Jim, 'I can't decide how I feel about this.' But before Jim had time to decide, they were off!

Whoosh! went the boat as it shot across the water. As they drifted further and further out to sea, the rain grew heavier and heavier and the wind blew harder and harder. Jim grew rather nervous that the seashore had become a little dot in the distance.

'We're casting the nets now, lad,' Charlie told Jim. He had to shout over the noise of the rain splashing against the sea.

Jim was keen to make a good impression and help in any way he could. 'I'll help!' he called, although what with the rain splooshing and splatting loudly all around them and the wind whooshing and whirring, Jim's voice got lost on the air and it sounded more like 'Help!'

Charlie looked at him disapprovingly. 'Now's not the time to panic, lad,' he said.

Jim could tell that Charlie thrived off his work as a fisherman. The stronger the weather became, the stronger Charlie became. He was a true fisherman, thought Jim, and so were all his friends. Nothing could stop them from doing their job. Jim wanted to be just like them and tried his best, but the more he tried, the more things seemed to go wrong. He tried to help when the fishermen cast their nets into the water, but got all tangled up in the nets and had to cry out for them to stop before they threw him in too. He tried to brighten things up when the weather got really bad by whistling a cheery whistle, but the fishermen quickly told him that whistling at sea was bad luck and if he knew what was good for him, he would stop right away.

He tried to put on a brave face when a storm came rolling through the skies but, in no time, found himself clinging desperately on to the side of the boat. Crack! went the lightning. Crash! went the thunder. 'Crikey!' went Jim.

At long last, when the boat reached the seashore, Jim was only too relieved to be back on dry land. Night had broken into morning and the early birds were feasting on their breakfasts. The fishermen had caught many herrings and the trip had been a success. But, for Jim, it had been a disaster. He sat down, dejected, on the ground.

'Oh dear, that trial didn't go very well. I suppose I can't have a job as a fisherman now.'

'Never mind, lad,' Charlie said. 'I'm afraid you don't have what it takes to be a fisherman, but the point is, everyone could see that you tried. Trying is the important thing. Just you keep up the spirit of trying, you'll find there's something out there for you.'

'I hope so,' sighed Jim. 'In the meantime, I suppose it's back to jumping and whistling for me.'

'What's that?' Charlie asked, curious.

'That's how I earn money,' Jim said. 'I whistle like … well, I won't show you if it's bad luck near the sea and I also jump … like this!' He jumped up in the air, a great big, high jump, so high he even shot up above Charlie's head.

'That's fantastic!' Charlie exclaimed when Jim had landed back on the ground.

'I'd prefer to have a proper job,' Jim said.

'But that's just it,' said Charlie. 'You could have one! They could really use those jumping skills at the Tower Curing Works. That's where the herrings are taken next. Your jumping skills would come in useful at the smoke house because … well, I'll show you. Follow me.'

Jim followed Charlie to the Tower Curing Works, all the while wondering what jumping could possibly have to do with all this. As they walked, Charlie explained to Jim what happened in the smoke house. 'First the herrings are soaked in brine, which is very salty water. The next stop is the smoke house where the herrings are put on speats, which are long sticks, and are hung in rows from a very high ceiling. Sawdust and chippings are placed on the ground beneath the herrings, on which a fire is lit. The smoke from the fire rises up towards the herrings. This is called smoking and it's what gives the herrings a nice smoky flavour and makes them stay fresh for longer.'

When they arrived at the smoke house, Jim saw that it was just as Charlie had described. Inside, sawdust and chippings were placed in a pile on the ground on which a fire would later be lit. He could smell a nice smoky smell; it reminded him of the fires he would light outside his wooden box on winter evenings. It was a very comforting smell. Jim looked up to see that above them were endless rows of wooden beams from which hung the herrings. The ceiling was so high that it seemed to go on, and on, and on, forever, up and up and up, herring after herring after herring. 'A sky full of herrings,' thought Jim.

He then noticed a curious sight. A man sprang up to one of the lower beams. He had a bunch of herrings in one hand and, with his other hand, he hoisted himself up then spread his legs out through the air so that each leg landed on an opposite beam. Following this, he shimmied his way up the beams, each leg pushing against a beam. Jim watched, fascinated, as the man disappeared higher and higher into the sky full of herrings. He couldn't help but feel that it looked rather fun and he wouldn't mind giving it a go himself.

'His legs are splayed out, you see, so that he can climb up and reach the very high beams to hang the herrings.' Charlie explained. 'It's tricky work, and he has to be strong of the arms and sure of the foot so as not to lose his balance. But with your jumping skills, lad, it may not be too difficult.'

'Easy!' cried Jim. He jumped up in the air and caught hold of a very high beam. While he was swinging from the beam, he spread

out his legs, one foot on each opposite beam, just as the man had done, and he worked his way swiftly upwards. Jim heard clapping and cheering from below him. He looked down and saw that a small crowd of the workers had gathered beneath him and were very impressed. Jim spent the rest of the day working in the smoke house, using his jumping skills to help hang the herrings on the high beams.

By the end of the day he had a job, a real job as a worker in the smoke house. Jim saved his earnings, and after a time he was able to buy his very own house. No more wooden boxes for Jim; this house had proper windows, a door through which he could walk instead of crawl and – who'd have thought it, folks? – a real chimney. Inside the house was a bed to rest his head and a bath to wash himself.

But a house wasn't the only good thing to come out of Jim's new job at the smoke house. He really enjoyed going to work every day. The people he worked with were very friendly, and even though the work was hard, some days tough, it felt like they were all in it together and nothing got Jim through a difficult day like feeling he was surrounded by friends. He quickly became very popular because he could whistle any song he was asked to, although he still liked the jolly songs best. He earned the nickname 'Jumping Jim' and it felt wonderful that he could use his jumping skills to help people.

Sometimes in the evening everyone would gather round a campfire together, laugh, tell jokes and play games. Often Charlie would join them and tell interesting stories about the day he'd just had at sea. Jim discovered that he was a brilliant cook on those campfire nights and would cook any meal you asked him to, provided that meal was herrings. As he listened to Charlie's stories and tucked into his herrings, surrounded by good company, Jim felt so glad that he had kept trying, even when things weren't working out for him. He realised that if Charlie hadn't seen he was trying, he may not have recommended him for a job at the smoke house and he would have missed out on finding what fast became his – well – *home*. He was surrounded by people who cared about him and he cared about them too. After all, Jim would tell you, a house can be made from *anything*, from shoes or sticks or bits of string. If it has walls and a ceiling, it's still a house. But a *home* is a place where you are surrounded by people who care about you. It doesn't matter where in the world this home is, how big or small, as long as the people who care about you are there.

And Jim had found his home in a sky full of herrings …

Now you are at the end of this story, you can understand the beginning, and so the only thing left to be said is, 'the end'.

The end.

5

ISOLDE OF THE ICENI

INSPIRED BY LYNN MUSEUM

In the Story – The Silver Coins

*O*nce upon a time, there lived a girl called Courage. Well, actually her real name was Isolde, but she insisted that everyone called her Courage because, more than anything else in the world, she wanted to truly live up to that name. This is a story about how she did just that.

To begin this story, you will have to step back in time – go on, stretch your legs and step back, thousands and thousands of years. Step back a bit further, now even further, back to ancient Britain – goodness, that was a great big step back! Now that our feet are miles apart because we've stepped back so far, we have arrived in a time called the Iron Age. Let's take a look at Iron Age Norfolk where Courage lived.

Here we are, in the middle of a luscious green patch of land. All around us are fields and forests as far as the eye can see. We are surrounded by roundhouses where lots of people live together. These days, we call an Iron Age settlement such as this an 'oppidum'. The people who live in this oppidum are part of the Iceni tribe. The Iceni work as farmers; they love nature, respect the land they farm and look after the animals they keep – horses, cows, goats and sheep. Can you spot that cow taking a drink from a pool of water? And look, there goes an Iceni farmer on his horse, off on a journey. You see, this is not the only oppidum in Norfolk. There are lots of other oppida (that's lots of oppidums) dotted about the land and, often, the Iceni farmers travel from one oppidum to another to trade cows and sheep in exchange for food.

Now, there is one very important thing you must know about the time in which Courage lived. There's been a bit of a shake-up recently, to the way things normally are, because some of the Iceni have left the oppidum to go and fight in battles. The battles they are fighting are against the Romans, who rule much of ancient Britain. The Romans have taken some of the Iceni land and because the Iceni don't think this is fair, many of them have got together to rise up in rebellion – and make no mistake about it, they mean business! The leader of this rebellion is a fearsome woman called Boudica. You might have heard stories about how she is a brave and fierce warrior who takes no nonsense and rides a chariot drawn by horses, her long, red hair flowing in the wind.

The Iceni who follow Boudica into battle don't have fancy swords and shields like the Romans. Instead they have made themselves spears, long sticks with sharp, pointy ends. These spears are made from iron; it wasn't called the Iron Age for nothing, you know!

Now that you have learned lots of exciting things about the time Courage lived in, it's time to meet Courage herself. Here she comes, charging through the oppidum on her white horse. Courage is certainly much too young to go and fight in battles, but she's heard all about Boudica and wants to be just like her. Look, she's made herself a little pretend spear from a branch of hazel wood.

'My name is Courage!' she cries, because she wants to truly live up to that name.

Let's begin our story of how she did just that.

'My name is Courage, get out of my way!'

People certainly did get out of her way. As soon as they saw Courage galloping on her horse, they all scattered in different directions.

'Look out, here comes Courage!' The children ran away because they were scared of Courage, she was so fierce. They didn't like the way she shouted at them and bossed them about.

As for the grown-ups, they avoided her because they thought she was a nuisance. Sometimes, they would roll their eyes as soon as they saw her. 'Oh no, here comes Courage. What a nuisance!'

When she was charging on her horse, Courage felt very big and powerful, but when she was stomping about on her feet, she liked to prove she was equally big and powerful by starting fights. Courage was very strong and could take on anyone, not that anyone wanted to take on Courage!

However, there were other times, when Courage wanted to join in with what people were doing. She tried to play with the other children and join in with their games, but they ran away. 'Oh no, she's going to start a fight, run!'

She tried to join in with the grown-ups doing their chores, like washing or carrying firewood, but they told her to 'go away, go on, get out, you nuisance!'

Courage couldn't understand why people were never happy to see her, she thought they should have been grateful to have someone so daring, tough and bold amongst them. Sometimes, the fact that nobody wanted her around felt a bit hurtful. One morning, she decided to ask her wise old grandmother what she could do to make people happy to see her. Courage adored her grandmother and thought she must be the cleverest woman in all the world because she always knew the answers to everything.

Now, whenever Courage made a decision to do something, she acted on it very quickly without much thought, and that morning when she decided to ask her grandmother a question, it was no different. Courage bolted straight to her grandmother's roundhouse and burst through the door like an explosion of fire.

'Grandmother, it's me! I've come to ask you a question!'

Grandmother was chopping carrots for a stew. She didn't look up when Courage burst through the door but continued to chop. 'Yes, I knew it was you straight away because you shouted.'

Courage bounded up to Grandmother, full of admiration and enthusiasm for her. 'Grandmother, why do the children run away and the grown-ups tell me I'm a nuisance whenever I try to join in?'

'Well,' Grandmother said, 'think about the way you behave. You have courage, but how do you use it? Charge about on a horse like you own the world? Shout at people? Start fights? That doesn't make you brave, it makes you a bully!'

'But if I don't do those things then how am I supposed to truly live up to my name?' asked Courage.

'Learn how to use your courage wisely,' said

Grandmother. 'Once you know how to do that then you will truly live up to your name.'

'Oh, Grandmother!' cried Courage. 'You are very wise, you must surely know how I can use my courage wisely. Won't you tell me, right now?'

Grandmother smiled a knowing smile, 'Ah yes, I can tell you, but not right now. First, I have a task for you. Pay attention now, it's important. I have some silver coins and I want you to take them to the Iceni people who live in the roundhouses on the other side of the forest. You should be able to get there and back in a day if you ride on your horse. These silver coins will go towards helping Boudica and her battle, so the task is a special one. That's why I've entrusted it to you.'

'It sounds like an adventure!' cried Courage. 'But, oh Grandmother, can't you tell me how to use my courage wisely before I go? Why do I have to wait till I get back?'

'Because that's the way it is,' Grandmother said.

Courage was impatient and felt annoyed

that she had to wait till she got back. 'Very well, Grandmother,' she thought. 'If you won't tell me how to use my Courage wisely right away, then I'll use this task to prove that I don't need to be told! I know what I'll do, I'll take my wooden spear with me and use it to fight someone! I'm bound to meet someone on the way through the forest whom I can fight. That way, I'll show everyone that I already know how to truly live up to my name. I don't need you to tell me how to do that!'

Courage fastened her wooden spear to her side. She made ready her white horse for the journey. His name was Prasutagus, a very loyal and friendly horse, named after Boudica's husband. Grandmother gave Courage the silver coins in a cloth bag and waved her off as she rode into the forest. Off went Courage through the trees, strong as the wind, swift as the breeze. She had a horse, a wooden spear, some silver coins and a chance to truly live up to her name.

It was a beautiful day in the forest; the air was crisp and clear and the sunlight glistened through the trees. Above the tree tops in the blue skies, Courage saw pure white clouds. Some of them were shaped like things she recognised and she had fun pointing them out to Prasutagus. 'There's a cloud shaped like a man with a spear, that one's shaped like a star, that one's shaped like a baby, that one's shaped like a flower and, oh, look at that one in the distance … it's shaped just like a sheep!' She laughed. 'It looks like a silly sheep standing on a rock, afraid to jump down.'

But as they drew closer to the cloud, Courage realised that it wasn't a cloud at all.

'Wait a second, it IS a silly sheep standing on a rock afraid to jump down!'

The sheep had the roundest, fluffiest body you ever did see, from which protruded four little legs with tiny hooves. The rock he was standing on was very tall and the sheep was staring down over a sheer, sharp edge.

'Oh, you silly sheep, how did you get onto that tall rock?' Courage shouted at the sheep, but this only seemed to make him more upset and he gave a distressed bleat in response.

As shouting didn't seem to help, Courage jumped down from Prasutagus' back. 'My name is Courage, fear not, for I will save you! I know what I'll do, I'll climb up that rock and jump down with you. You won't be so afraid if we both jump together.'

Quickly, she began to scramble up the other side of the rock, which was bumpy and easy to climb with round stones to place her feet on. Once at the top next to the sheep, however, her stomach churned. Oh dear, oh dear, they were much higher up than she had originally assumed they would be, and oh dear, that drop down did look sheer and sharp. Courage felt altogether daunted and her knees began to wobble.

'On second thoughts,' she considered, 'perhaps jumping off a tall rock isn't the best idea.' She would have to think harder about how to save the sheep.

'My name is Courage and I don't know what to do … my name is … oh wait a second, I've been just as silly as you!' Courage realised that the sheep didn't need to jump down at all and nor, for that matter, did she. They could both climb down the other side of the rock, the bumpy side, just as she had climbed up.

'Turn around,' she instructed the sheep, 'and climb down the bumpy side of the rock with me.'

The sheep turned, but still appeared unsettled at the idea of climbing down. From her side, Courage took her wooden spear, the one she had brought to fight someone with and, with one end firmly in her hand, she reached out the other end towards the sheep. 'Take hold of this in your mouth,' she said. 'That way, I've got hold of you and I won't let you fall.'

The sheep clamped the other end of the wooden spear in his mouth. Then Courage led him gently down from the rock. It was a bit tricky, what with guiding the sheep, who was rather bulky, and Courage felt nervous she would trip, slip or slide. But then she reminded herself, 'My name is Courage!' and continued to climb down with determination.

When they were both standing on the grass at the bottom of the rock, the sheep was so happy to be safe that he started to jump about, ever so high, up and down, up and down. 'I think you'd better stay with me, you silly sheep,' said Courage, 'or else you might jump high enough to find yourself back up on that tall rock again!' And, with that, off went Courage through the trees, strong as the wind, swift as the breeze. She had a horse, a wooden spear, some silver coins, a silly sheep and a chance to truly live up to her name.

They hadn't been travelling for long when they came across a goat in the middle of a pool of water. The goat was white and fluffy with a long, anxious face and two large, sturdy horns which shot up from his head. He stood on a small mound of land in the middle of the pool. The water rose up to his hooves and he didn't seem happy about that at all. The goat bleated frantically as he looked about for a way to cross the water, but saw there was none.

'Oh, you giddy goat, however did you get yourself into the middle of the pool of water?' Courage shouted at the goat. Then she remembered that shouting didn't help, so she jumped down from Prasutagus' back. 'My name is Courage, fear not, for I will save you. I know what I'll do, I'll jump in the water and swim!'

Courage sprang towards the pool of water and was about to dive in when, just as she'd reached the water's edge, she stopped and took in the size of the pool. Oh dear, oh dear – the pool was as big as one of the roundhouses at home and that water looked very deep indeed.

'On second thoughts,' Courage considered, 'perhaps jumping into a pool of very deep water isn't the best idea.' She would have to think harder about how to save the goat. Courage looked around for inspiration and saw a large fallen branch lying on the ground, a good, sturdy one. She heaved and heaved and lifted the branch. Then Courage placed the branch across the water with one end at her feet, the other end on the mound by the goat's hooves.

'Look, I've made a bridge,' called Courage to the goat. 'Walk across it towards me.' But the goat was hesitant. When it became clear that he wasn't going to budge, Courage decided to go and get him. She began to walk carefully across the sturdy branch until she was next to the goat on the mound. 'Come on, I'll lead you back to the land.'

From her side, Courage took her wooden spear, the one she had brought to fight someone with, and with one end firmly in her hand, she reached out the other end towards the goat. 'Take hold of this in your mouth. That way, I've got hold of you and I won't let you fall.'

The goat clamped the other end of the spear in his mouth and Courage carefully led him across the branch over the water. It was a bit tricky, what with guiding a giddy goat, and as the branch wobbled, so did her nerves! But then she reminded herself, 'My name is Courage', and continued to walk with determination.

Once they were both standing on dry land, the goat was so happy to be safe that he started to jump about, ever so high, up and down, up and down. 'I think you'd better stay with me, you giddy goat,' said Courage. 'If I leave you, you'll probably jump about and fall in the water.'

Then, off went Courage through the trees, strong as the wind, swift as the breeze. She had a horse, a wooden spear, some silver coins, a silly sheep, a giddy goat and a chance to truly live up to her name.

They had been travelling for quite some time when they came across a cow stuck in the middle of a great patch of mud. The cow was brown and almost camouflaged with the mud as she was up to her knees in it. She looked very distressed, and as soon as she saw Courage, she started to 'moo!' desperately, as though asking for help.

'You cowardly cow, how did you get stuck in the middle of that mud?' Courage shouted at the cow. Then she remembered that shouting didn't help, so she jumped down from Prasutagus' back. 'My name is Courage, fear not, for I will save you. I know what I'll do, I'll jump in the mud and pull you to land!'

Courage hurtled towards the mud and was about to fling herself in, but just as she reached the mud's edge she stopped and thought about what she was doing. Oh dear, oh dear – the mud patch looked extremely deep. It was sticky mud, all thick and gloopy, boggy and bumpy like a great big bowl of mushy stew. The poor cow, Courage realised, couldn't move because her legs were stuck in the sticky, tricky mud. If she jumped in, she would get stuck too.

'On second thoughts,' Courage considered, 'perhaps propelling myself into a great big patch of sticky mud isn't the best idea.' She would have to think harder about how to save the cow. Unfortunately, there wasn't much time for thinking because, much to her horror, the cow started to sink in the mud.

'Moo!' went the cow, as she sank down further and further at a worrying speed. Courage lay down on her front so that her body was on dry land, but she could stretch her arms out over the mud. From her side, Courage took her wooden spear, the one she had brought to fight someone with and, with her hand firmly on one end, she reached out the other end to the cow. 'Take the other end in your mouth. That way, I've got hold of you and I won't let you sink!'

The cow clamped her mouth around the wooden spear.

'Now,' cried Courage, 'I'm going to pull you out!'

Courage pulled and pulled and pulled. For all that she was strong, she had her work cut out, because the cow was heavy and it would take all the strength and stamina she had to unstick her. Whenever she felt like she couldn't go on, she reminded herself, 'My name is Courage', and continued to pull with determination. Courage heaved and heaved and heaved until, finally, the cow started to budge.

'Now move your legs around, come on, move them and help yourself to get free from the mud, move, move!' Courage shouted. She knew that shouting didn't help, but at urgent times such as this, it seemed necessary. What's more, it worked, because the cow started to move her legs. As Courage pulled her with all her might, the cow wiggled and wriggled and jiggled her legs free until, finally, she could move through the mud. Courage gave one last pull and the cow jumped through the mud on to dry land.

Courage collapsed her arms to the ground, exhausted. For a moment, she lay there silent, eyes shut, feeling as though she could sleep for a hundred years. When gradually she opened her eyes, she was faced with a peculiar yet heart-warming sight. Her horse, the silly sheep, the giddy goat and the cowardly cow were all standing over her, gazing down. The cow gave her a gentle nudge and Courage realised that she was helping her to her feet. Courage felt rather weak as she stood up, but the cow bent down so that she could step on her back to mount Prasutagus. As she rode, quite slowly, through the forest, all the animals stayed close by, as though ready to catch Courage if she fell. After some time, she felt happy to pick up the pace again.

Then, off went Courage through the trees, strong as the wind, swift as the breeze. She had a horse, a wooden spear, some silver coins, a silly sheep, a giddy goat, a cowardly cow and a chance to truly live up to her name.

Courage could see the roofs of roundhouses in the distance, a relieving sight. They were nearly at their destination and she was looking forward to a nice rest and some food. But Courage's journey of challenges was not over, not yet. The group turned a corner and came across a creature, a very proud, alert creature sitting under a tree, stoic as can be, a creature with sharp eyes, sharp ears and even sharper teeth. It was a wolf.

Courage gasped, she had not seen a wolf in the flesh before, they never ventured into the oppidum, but this one certainly lived up to the stories she had heard about wolves – fierce, magnificent and not to be messed with. The Iceni greatly respected and revered wolves. Above all, they quite happily left them alone, thank you very much! Everyone knew that you shouldn't go near a wolf. Wolves have appetites and, oh yes, they bite! This wolf was clearly no exception. He sat very still and regal as they passed, but his eyes were alive as lightning and fixed unblinkingly on Courage and the animals.

There was no way they could reach the roundhouses without passing the wolf and – oh dear, oh dear – the animals were all very frightened. They shuddered and shook and looked down at their feet as they trundled forward.

'My name is Courage. Fear not, for I will save you. I know what I'll do, I'll fight the wolf!' After all, that's why she had brought her wooden spear in the first place. This was her chance, the chance she had been waiting for, her chance to truly live up to her name.

As they drew closer to the wolf, Courage narrowed her eyes. The wolf narrowed his eyes.

She gritted her teeth. The wolf gritted his teeth.

She clutched her wooden spear. The wolf scraped the ground with his paw.

The more she started something, the more he responded.

Thinking about it, Courage realised that it made sense to stop. 'On second thoughts,' considered Courage, 'perhaps starting a fight with a wolf is not the best idea. He seems to be sitting there quite happily, so I'll just let him be.' Courage continued to ride forward with determination towards the roundhouses, the animals safe at her side.

The wolf gave her a respectful nod as they passed. He was happy to let them go and it felt like she'd made the right decision. Then, why did she feel so guilty? Why did she feel so sad? Why did she feel as though she had let everyone down, most of all herself? Courage fought the tears in her eyes. She had missed her chance, the chance she had been waiting for, her chance

to truly live up to her name. She hadn't fought anyone on her journey. She couldn't prove to Grandmother that she knew how to use her courage wisely and truly live up to her name.

'My name is not Courage,' she said with a heavy heart. 'I have failed.'

When they arrived at the roundhouses, the animals were delighted to stay in a nice, friendly place. The Iceni people were very happy to receive the silver coins for Boudica. They prepared some delicious food for Courage and Prasutagus. But Courage didn't feel much like enjoying herself. She let Prasutagus enjoy his treats because he'd fully earned them, ate a little herself, to be polite, then said she needed to be on her way home.

Back through the forest, Courage didn't feel half as free or powerful as she usually felt when riding on her horse. When they finally arrived at Grandmother's roundhouse, Courage slumped through the door and burst into tears.

'My dear!' exclaimed Grandmother. 'Why are you crying? Did something bad happen on your journey?'

Courage explained to her grandmother, in great detail, everything that had happened. All about the silly sheep on the rock, the giddy goat in the water, the cowardly cow stuck in the mud and how she had rescued them with nothing but her wits and her wooden spear. Then she told her about the wolf and how she had decided not to fight him. 'So you see, Grandmother, I failed at my chance to truly live up to my name. I thought I could prove that you didn't need to tell me how to use my courage wisely but, as I'm sure you've realised, you really do.'

'But my dear!' cried Grandmother. 'I don't need to tell you anything at all. You've learned it all for yourself. Don't you see? You used your courage to save those animals from very difficult situations. You didn't rush in, you thought about what was best for everyone and still succeeded in being incredibly strong, brave and valiant. As for your wooden spear, you used it not to fight, but to help! Was there ever a wiser way to use courage?'

'But Grandmother,' said Courage, confused, 'if I am, as you say, incredibly strong, brave and valiant, then why didn't I prove that by fighting the wolf? I could have started a fight but I didn't.'

'Yes,' said Grandmother, 'you could have started a fight but you chose not to. You decided that it would be better to keep the peace, a wonderfully courageous and wise decision. Now you truly live up to your name, and I didn't have to tell you a thing!'

Courage was about to give a jump of joy when, just as her feet lifted from the ground, she stopped and thought. 'Do you know, Grandmother, now that I know I truly live up to my name of Courage, I think I would rather be called by my real name, Isolde. You see, I no longer feel the need to prove that I'm courageous because I know I am.'

'I think that's a wonderful idea,' said Grandmother.

Isolde was ecstatic. 'Oh, Grandmother, I'm so happy and exploding with energy, I'm going to go for a ride right now!'

'You little spark! I think you'd better eat something first.' Grandmother made her yummy stew and she ate three bowls full – well, she'd had a long and busy day.

Isolde was about to leave and fetch Prasutagus when, all of a sudden, Grandmother gave a scream and jumped up on her stool. 'Arghhh, a mouse!'

Isolde saw that there was indeed a little brown mouse with twitching whiskers and a flicking tail sitting by her stool. 'Oh, Grandmother!' she giggled. 'That little mouse is just as scared of you as you are of it. Don't let your fear keep you on that stool all day, look him square in the eyes and politely show him the door.'

'Oh,' sighed Grandmother, 'if my grand-daughter can be so courageous then so can I!' With a tremble, she got down from the stool, walked to the door, opened it, turned to the little mouse, looked him square in the eyes and with a frightened squeak mumbled, 'Here is the door, could you kindly go through it please?'

The little mouse did just that.

Grandmother laughed. 'Well,' she said, 'it seems that just as you have learned some wisdom, I have learned some courage. Now, I suggest you go for a ride soon before it gets dark.'

But there was no need to suggest it. Isolde had already sped off to fetch Prasutagus, her brilliant horse. Then, off they went through the trees, strong as the wind, swift as the breeze, and, oh yikes, here she comes now! Can you see her, charging towards us, brave and bold as can be? She's looking for people she can help.

'My name is Isolde! Can I help you?'

This time, the children don't run away in fright and the grown-ups don't think she's a nuisance. In fact, they all look very happy to see her, very happy indeed.

Here comes Isolde! Hooray! She's going to save the day!

6

THE CURIOUS KITTEN AND THE WONDERFUL WATCH

INSPIRED BY ANCIENT HOUSE MUSEUM

In the Story – The Elizabethan Hall, a First World War Kitchen and Tudor Garden

Once upon a time, there lived a little kitten. But no, that isn't quite the right way to begin.

Oh, the fact that there was a little kitten is entirely correct, rather, 'once upon a time' isn't quite true. This story should begin with 'once upon *many* times'. You see, this little kitten travelled through time. She saw many times, many, many times and so 'once upon many times', there lived a time-travelling little kitten.

Now this little kitten had to start somewhere before she time travelled and, as it happened, she started over a hundred years ago on the streets of Thetford, in Norfolk. A street kitten, she was born a stray – she didn't have a home or a family and had never been given a name. She was used to life on the streets and had no problem with finding food. It's fair to say that passers-by or occupants of the houses or shops she wandered into found her adorable and gave her a bowl of this, or a saucer of that, and so there was plenty of milk for our kitten.

When she saw her reflection in puddles on the ground, she observed that she was a little black ball of fluff with delicate white paws, sparkling green eyes, tiny ears which shot up straight like blades of grass and a bonny button nose with soft whiskers. She fancied that her name could be 'Bright Paws' or 'Emerald Eyes' or 'Wispy Whiskers' – until the day she found out what her real name was.

Before we find out about that, it needs to be said that this kitten was full to bursting with curiosity, as curious a kitten as ever you came across, and be sure that as soon as you came across her she would ask you a question. 'Where does this path lead?' 'What's that?' 'How does it work?' 'Does it talk?' 'Who are you?' 'Are you my friend?' 'What's that?' 'How old is it?' 'Where does it come from?' 'What's this?' 'Can I eat it?' Always searching, never still, travelling where curiosity took her.

One day, curiosity took her into a baker's shop where the baker's daughter greeted her. 'Oh, hello, you must be curious!'

'Yes,' our kitten thought, 'I suppose I must be.'

And that's how Curious came by her real name.

Curious by name, curious by nature, Curious travelled where curiosity took her. Day by day, Curious continued in this way, up and down the streets of Thetford until, one day, curiosity took her to a shop, a shop which changed her life forever.

The shop caught her eye as she passed by on the street. The first thing that struck her was that the building was very distinctive and beautiful, the walls were striped black and white and there was a large bay window at the front. The window was full of watches and clocks. Now, you may well know what a watch or a clock looks like, but Curious had never seen one and had no idea what they were used for. She stared in wonder at the round clock faces with their circles of numbers and two dials, a big one and a little one, which elegantly passed each number with a soft 'tick tock'.

A circle of numbers and a ticking thing – what could it be? Curious supposed that the ticking thing must be measuring something as it passed each number, although she could never have guessed that the thing it was measuring was time.

The ticking objects were an altogether fascinating sight and she wanted to find out more. Curious by name, Curious by nature, Curious travelled where curiosity took her, inside the shop. The shop had a nice, musty smell and a real sense of mystery and intrigue hovered in the air. As soon as Curious stepped inside she felt as though something magical was about to happen. The shop was empty, there was no one around and all she could hear was the gentle orchestra of tick, tock, tick, tock, played by the many, many ticking objects.

There was one in particular which stood out and took her fancy, a beautiful ticking object that rested on top of a table. Curious pounced nimbly up on the table to get a better look at it.

It wasn't that this ticking object appeared particularly different from the others, but there was something about it, something different, something special, something that Curious couldn't quite put her paw on – but put her paw on it she did, nonetheless, if only to feel how smooth an object it was. 'What are you, ticking object?' she asked. 'Please show me what you are.'

All of a sudden, before Curious knew what was happening the ticking object sprang up into the air and began to shake vigorously, emitting strange, bright sparks of light as it shook. Curious darted back with surprise as the sparks shot through the air, fast as lightning, with a whoosh, whizz, whirr and watch this!

No sooner had it begun than it stopped, in what seemed like seconds. Astonished, Curious looked around her to see that she was somewhere completely different, although she hadn't moved at all. It seemed to her that she must be in exactly the same spot, but oh, what a

different spot it was. For one thing, she wasn't on
a table any more but on the floor. Curious gaped
around her to see that she wasn't in a shop and
there certainly weren't any more ticking objects.
The room was vast and grand.

The wall directly in front of her was covered with a magnificent draping of bright red and yellow stripes. Across the draping hung three very beautiful paintings. The painting in the middle was of a man on a horse and the two paintings on either side of him were of women wearing elegant dresses with big ruffs around their necks. Curious had never seen anyone wearing clothes of that style before, but she thought they looked very fancy. Underneath the paintings stood a splendid table with lots of food. It looked as though whoever lived in the house was about to eat a delicious feast.

Curious cast her eyes further across the room and saw a great fireplace. She would have loved to have curled up on a rug in front of that fireplace. It seemed to Curious that this room must be a very happy and warm place where people gathered together, what with the fireplace and feast. Tick, tock, tick, tock. Curious looked down to see that the ticking object was beside her on the floor.

'Here we are in the same room hundreds of years ago.'

Curious jumped back as a soft, magical voice came from the ticking object. 'This time was called the Elizabethan Age because Queen Elizabeth the First sat on the throne.'

'Goodness!' thought Curious, 'what an informative, magical ticking object you are! I had better listen if I'm to learn anything.'

'Back then, this room was a very important part of the family household. See how the table is generously laid with food, ready for a family meal.'

'Yes, it is,' thought Curious, 'and I wouldn't mind a taste of something.' She skipped up to the table, but no sooner had her paws left the floor than whoosh, whizz, whirr and watch this!

Once again, Curious looked around to see that she was somewhere completely different. This time, she was in a kitchen, busy, bright and bustling with lots of people. Curious had landed on the middle of a table covered with food, the ticking object at her side. She picked it up in her teeth and scurried to the corner so as not to be seen. She hid behind a tall tin object, which appeared to be used for washing as a woman was dipping a cloth in and out of the tin and wringing through the water.

Curious gazed at the food-covered table where she had been sitting. Across from the table was a fireplace and stove on which sat lots of pots, clearly cooking something nice. In front of her was a tall cupboard of vibrant yellow with red, white and blue bunting hanging from the top. Lots of plates and tea cups were stacked on the shelves of the cupboard as well as other objects such as a butter dish and brushes for cleaning. Next to the cupboard, sitting on a chair, was a tall man in a khaki uniform. Curious had never seen a uniform like that before and wondered why he was wearing it. She hoped the ticking object could tell her.

'We have visited the past of this house. Now we are in the same house in the future,' said the soft, magical voice from the ticking object.

Curious was mesmerised at the thought of being in the future and was very keen to hear what the ticking object had to say.

'Here we are in the kitchen where lots of people are hard at work. This is the time of the First World War. You see that man in the khaki uniform? He is a soldier. Lots of soldiers who fought in the war would have worn uniforms like that. War was a difficult time for everyone but, see here, in this kitchen, everyone has come together to help each other out. This house was often a place used for the purpose of helping people.'

'I do like to be in a busy kitchen full of people,' thought Curious. 'I would like to curl up by that fireplace. I should feel very comfortable with all these people around me.'

But, no sooner had she stepped out from behind the tin than whoosh, whizz, whirr and watch this!

Now she was in a garden, a beautiful garden bursting with fresh, luscious greenery and bright red flowers.

'We are at the same house, but back in the past again,' explained the soft, magical voice of the ticking object from beside her. 'This is a traditional Tudor garden. It was very well loved and looked after.'

'It looks lovely,' thought Curious, 'and I certainly wouldn't mind jumping in that greenery to play.' She pounced towards it, but no sooner had her paws left the ground than … whoosh, whiz, whir and watch this!

She was right back where she had started, in the shop sitting on a table next to the ticking object. It just sat there, simply, quietly and still, as though nothing had happened at all. Curious noted that everything around her was just as before and the shop's mysterious silence was broken only by the gentle orchestra of ticking objects all around her – tick, tock, tick, tock.

All of a sudden, Curious heard footsteps, and she glided quickly down from the table to hide. But not quickly enough.

'Hello,' a voice greeted her. 'I see you there, little kitten.'

It was a warm, friendly voice and Curious looked up from under the table to see a tall man wearing smart clothes.

'My name is Mr Kemp, I'm the Watchmaker. I see you've been admiring this very wonderful watch.' He picked up the ticking object from the table and bent down to hold it in front of her. So that's what it's called, thought Curious, a watch!

'Do you know what a watch is for?' asked Mr Kemp.

'An object that makes you travel through time,' thought Curious.

'A watch is an object which measures time,' explained Mr Kemp. 'As you go about your day, you look at your watch to see what time it is. You see the number where the big hand is pointing and the number where the little hand is pointing and that's how you tell the time.'

'That sounds interesting,' thought Curious, 'but nothing like this watch which just took me on a time-travelling adventure.'

'I made all these watches myself,' said Mr Kemp. 'But this one is different from the others. I have it on authority that this particular watch can take you backward and forward in time to show you this house throughout the ages. But it will only show those who have the curiosity to ask.'

'So, he knows about the watch,' thought Curious, excited. 'And the watch only showed me because I had the curiosity to ask. I knew that being curious was a good thing!'

'Now,' Mr Kemp tapped his finger on the watch, 'you see here that the big hand is pointing to twelve and the little hand is pointing to twenty. That means it's twenty past twelve and roundabout time we have some lunch. I'll get you a saucer of milk.'

'Hooray!' thought Curious, what a perfect end to her adventure.

After that day, Curious stayed in Mr Kemp's watchmaker's shop where she had milk and fish every day and never had to go back on the streets again, unless curiosity took her there. Mr Kemp was happy for her to live in his shop. She was a real hit with the customers. Better yet, the wonderful watch was there whenever she felt like going on a time-travelling adventure – which she did, many, many times.

One day, two children, a brother and a sister, came into the shop with their parents. The children were so beguiled by the wonderful watch that they came back to look at it the next day. Curious decided that it was time for her to stop time travelling and let other people have a chance. It felt right that such an exciting opportunity to see amazing things should be shared, and she was sure that the children would have the curiosity to ask.

And so it was that Curious chose to stay in the time where she felt most at home, in the watchmaker's shop with Mr Kemp. Curious by name, curious by nature, Curious travelled where curiosity took her, through time – many, many times – until she found her home, her very own 'once upon *a* time'.

The curious thing about this story is that if you want to go on the same time-travelling adventure as Curious, you don't need a wonderful watch at all! You can visit Ancient House Museum and see all that Curious saw, and more …

7

GREY SKIES AND SILVER LININGS

INSPIRED BY GRESSENHALL FARM AND WORKHOUSE

In the Story – The Door with the Clenched Fist Knocker, a Bath and Peg Dolls, the School Room, Laundry and Dungeon

Once upon a time, there lived a boy called Joe – but not a fairy-tale beginning for him, oh no, rather a beginning of woe.

Times were tough for Joe, but don't worry, this is a tale of finding rainbows amongst stormy skies, a tale of making friends during hard times, and there's lots of joy and sunshine to come. But, of course, Joe doesn't know that yet. We're still at the bleak beginning, and so, if you have a blanket, now would be a good time to snuggle.

Joe lived hundreds of years ago in the time of Queen Victoria, a time when things were very different from how they are today. Joe grew up in the Norfolk countryside with his close family, which sounds a treat, but unfortunately it wasn't. You see, Joe's family were very poor. They didn't have much to call their own except each other. There was Mum, Dad, Joe, who was nine, and his younger sister Lucy, who was six. There was also Lucy's little peg doll called Nancy, and Lucy gave her so much love that Nancy became part of the family.

The family lived on a farm and would have been known as agricultural labourers, which meant they worked very hard to help keep the farm in order and make things grow. They lived what you might call 'hand to mouth', which meant that, no sooner had their hands touched the food they had grown, they would eat it, then set their hands to work again to make more food grow. The family lived in a tiny cottage, a tumbled down, crumbled down, 'oh crikey is it going to fall down?' type of cottage with a rickety roof and a wonky old chimney. It was so small there was only one bedroom for everyone to sleep in, all squished and squashed together. The grown-ups huddled in a single bed and the children slept on straw on the floor.

Now, as you can imagine, the floor wasn't a very comfy place to sleep, but Joe didn't know any different and he liked being all snuggly with Lucy beside him, who was always curled up with Nancy. For what it was worth, Joe was very content with what he had and gave no mind to what he didn't have. However, little did Joe know that soon he would have nothing at all, nothing whatsoever, not a blanket, not a feather, not so much as a straw on the floor

– nothing at all – not even a pot to put nothing in – absolutely nothing! One very harsh and frosty winter, nothing on the farm grew and so there was nothing to eat, nothing! Joe's family were told to leave the farm because there was no work for them.

Without work and food, the family had no choice but to roam outside where it was cold enough to freeze your socks off, even though they didn't have any socks. Being so poor, they didn't even have shoes! The family walked barefoot, clothed only in tattered rags which didn't keep them warm at all. With a heavy heart, Dad announced that they were destitute and must go to the Workhouse. Joe didn't know what the Workhouse was, but he didn't much like the sound of it. The name 'Workhouse' didn't exactly sound like a barrel of laughs.

Dad explained that this was a place where poor people went when they had nothing and needed a roof over their heads and food in their tummies. Joe liked the idea of a roof and food, but he was petrified about being somewhere different. He didn't know what to expect. First, the family had to go and see the local Relieving Officer to ask for permission to enter the Workhouse. 'You can't just show up to the Workhouse or they won't let you in,' Dad explained. 'You have to prove that you really do have nothing and no choice but to be there. The Relieving Officer will listen to what you have to say about your situation and decide whether you have the right to enter the Workhouse.'

No sooner had Joe entered the room of the Relieving Officer than he wanted to leave. What a mean man, asking Mum and Dad lots of gruelling questions about their situation. Joe felt small and intimidated with that mean man looking down his nose at them. He didn't like feeling as though he and his family were a right nuisance. Mum and Dad did all the talking. Lucy kept her head low and clutched Nancy close to her the whole time.

Finally, the mean man said they could go to the Workhouse. He gave Dad a very important piece of paper which said the family were allowed entry, a paper not to be lost or they would all pay the cost, and Dad carried that very important piece of paper as though it were gold. Then the family walked for miles and miles on their bare feet to get to the Workhouse.

They arrived at a huge building, very different from the tiny cottage, about one hundred times the size, large and imposing. The big building was a grim sight through all the frost, so grim that Joe couldn't help but think it looked a bit like a prison. At the front of the building was a green door. On the green door was a knocker, a rather striking and spooky-looking knocker, shaped like a clenched fist. Joe gulped at the sight of that clenched fist knocker, so severe in appearance that it seemed to say 'knock at your peril'.

As Dad raised his hand to knock, Joe wanted to shout, 'No, don't!'

But it was too late. Knock. Knock. Knock.

The door creaked slowly open and there stood a tall man with a red beard.

'That's the porter,' Mum whispered to Joe.

'Have you got your paper?' the porter asked straight away. He seemed agitated, like he didn't have much time. Dad handed the very important piece of paper to the porter, who looked at it, sniffed and nodded.

'Come in then.'

The family walked tentatively through the green door. Lucy looked scared and clutched Nancy close to her. As the porter closed the door behind them, Joe took one last look at the clenched fist knocker and wondered when he would see the outside of that door again. The porter took the family to a little room called the Receiving Ward, where they were told they would have to wait for a medical inspection.

As they walked into the room, the porter asked Joe some questions. Despite being a bit irritable, Joe could tell the porter wasn't a nasty man, he just wanted to get on with his job without any bother.

'Now why do you keep scratching your head like that?' the porter asked him.

Joe realised he'd been scratching his head all day, although he supposed that must be because he was incredibly nervous. 'I don't know,' he replied to the porter. His voice was very quiet and his lips trembled as he spoke.

'How old are you?' the porter asked.

'Nine,' said Joe. He could just about remember his own age, in spite of the day's confusion.

'Nine,' repeated the porter. 'Old enough to be separated from your family.'

Separated! Joe could hardly believe what he had heard. He had to be in the Workhouse without his family, on his own! This was terrible news and Joe wanted to cry. But he could see Lucy was all upset and afraid, and he worried that if he started crying that would make Lucy cry too. He didn't want her to feel frightened and so, as bravely as he could, Joe kept a straight face and acted like everything was alright. But he didn't feel alright, oh dear, not at all!

The family waited and waited and waited for what felt like many hours for the Medical Officer. Joe didn't know how long exactly, only that daylight was dwindling and as the darkness grew so did Joe's feeling of despair about what was to come, although he kept his brave face on for Lucy's sake.

At last the Medical Officer arrived. He wasn't too scary, rather friendly in fact. As he examined each member of the family he explained that he was looking for 'the itch'. Joe had heard of 'the itch' before, it was a horrible thing which meant you got very itchy skin. Every time the Medical Officer said 'the itch', Joe's head felt all tingly and he scratched it. The Medical Officer saw that Joe kept scratching his head and went to have a look at it. 'Oh no!' thought Joe, 'What if I have the itch?'

'It's not the itch,' said the Medical Officer, 'it's nits!'

Joe was extremely relieved that he had nits and not 'the itch'. He knew that nits were very common and the Medical Officer would have to shave his head. Joe didn't mind that. Better than having nits!

Once Joe's head was shaved, the Medical Officer told the family that they had all passed their medical inspection and could go on to have a bath. Joe had never had a proper bath before and, after the day's ordeals, thought it sounded rather a nice, comforting idea. That is, until he actually saw the bath. There was only one bath and everyone who entered the Workhouse that day got in it, sharing the same bath water. Lots of people had arrived that day and they all had to wait in a line for the bath. By the time it was Joe's turn, the bath was full of dirty old, cloudy old, stinky old water. Not nice! But Joe was told he must have a bath and that was that, so in he went. Yuck!

Next, Joe and his family were given new clothes and their old tatters were taken away.

Joe was dressed in a shirt, trousers and woollen jacket with shoes, real shoes, on his feet! Lucy was dressed in a blue gingham dress with a flannel petticoat, a shawl and a white cap. They both looked very smart. Joe had never worn clothes like this before and they felt stiff and strange, but, oh, it was so good to be much warmer. Now came the time that he had been bracing himself for. Joe was separated from his family and had to go it alone in the Workhouse.

The whole family were taken in different directions. Dad had to go one way, Mum another. Joe was relieved to see that Lucy was allowed to stay with Mum because she was only six. Joe watched Lucy walk away holding Mum's hand with Nancy in her other hand and his heart warmed. They were still together, and that was that. But no, unfortunately, that was not that. The porter came along and said that Lucy couldn't keep Nancy. All the family's possessions had to be taken away and that included peg dolls! But she's not just a peg doll, she's part of the family! Nancy, oh no! Joe watched in horror as Lucy had Nancy plucked from her arms. She burst out crying, but the porter just walked away holding Nancy in his hand with no care at all. Joe was so frustrated that he couldn't do anything to help or comfort Lucy, he just had to watch her walk away crying. It was horrible.

The family's introduction to the Workhouse had taken all day and now it was bedtime, his first bedtime alone without Lucy snuggled by his side. Joe was taken to the boys' dormitory. Lots of beds were lined in rows across the room. Joe had never been in a real bed before and supposed that he should be grateful. After all, it was much nicer than sleeping on straw on the floor. But at least then he had been surrounded by his family, the people who loved him. Now he was all alone.

Joe stared at the ceiling and an image flashed through his mind, the image of Lucy getting Nancy taken away. He felt a lump in his stomach like he wanted to cry, but he held it all in. Joe looked round at the boys in the rows of beds beside him and wondered if they were asleep or just staring at the ceiling, same as him.

Dong! Dong! Dong! Joe was startled awake from his night of dozing off and on by the sound of a loud bell. 'Doesn't it know we can all hear it?' thought Joe. He would soon get used to the sound of that dong every morning. It signalled the beginning of his day in the Workhouse, which went like this:

First there was breakfast. Breakfast, you say, hooray! Eggs and beans on toast, or porridge or fruit, you say? No, don't be silly, this was the Workhouse, no yummy breakfast here, you'll eat gruel. Gruel was like very, very runny porridge with no flavour. Gloopy, gooey, gruesome gruel! Eat it all up now!

Then it was time for school. School, you say, hooray! Time to make friends and learn all sorts of exciting things about the world around us. No, don't be silly, this was the Workhouse, you'll sit at a desk and be quiet, or you'll be in a lot of trouble. You'll learn reading, writing and arithmetic and don't you forget what you've learned or you'll be in trouble for that too!

Then it was playtime. Playtime, you say, hooray! Time to run around, play games and have lots of fun! No, don't be silly, this was the Workhouse, no fun here! You can stand about in the yard, stretch your legs a bit and, if you're very lucky, play on the swing after you've waited your turn, if you get a turn at all.

These may not sound like things that you would feel particularly jolly about, but let's find out how Joe felt about all this. You have to remember that Joe wasn't used to any of these things. He'd grown up cold, hungry and without an education. Yes, the gruel was yucky, but Joe hadn't eaten for a long time and he was very grateful to have food in his belly even if it was like eating sloppy old sludge. School, although strict, was a wonderful thing for Joe. He knew he would never have had the opportunity to go to school if he had stayed working on the farm, and now here he sat in a real classroom with other boys. He enjoyed learning the three Rs – Reading, 'Riting and 'Rithmetic – as well as history and geography with maps. He especially loved to see how letters made up the words he spoke.

The teacher, Mr Bradfield, took no nonsense so the boys gave none. They listened up and learned their lessons. They were going to leave that Workhouse educated young men and that was an exciting thought. As for playtime, this was really fun for Joe. He didn't know any boys his own age back on the farm and now he was surrounded by them. On his first day, Joe quickly made good friends with two boys called Christopher and Edward, or Chris and Ed, who came and chatted to him as the boys stood in the yard. Chris and Ed had both been in the Workhouse for some time and were able to answer lots of Joe's burning questions about what his family might be doing in the Workhouse.

'Your sister will go to school too,' said Ed. 'She'll learn reading, writing and arithmetic as well as needlework and knitting.'

'I bet Lucy will be good at learning in school!' said Joe, overjoyed that Lucy also got an education. He was sure she would be bright as a button.

'Your mum,' Ed continued, 'will be working in the laundry. Don't know much about it other than it's hot, sweaty and stinky. Tough working in there.'

'Mum's a hard worker and used to tough work on a farm,' said Joe, 'I know she'll be alright.'

'Your dad,' said Chris, eager to join in, 'will be doing jobs like picking oakum. That means your dad will be given old rope and has to untwist it into strands. Picking oakum is very hard on the hands, makes your skin all dry, cracked and sore.'

'That sounds tough,' said Joe, 'tedious too.'

'It is tedious,' said Chris. 'But it keeps you busy, that's the point. You're not supposed to enjoy yourself in the Workhouse, you're supposed to work.'

'And does everyone do the same things every day?' asked Joe.

'Same every day,' said Ed.

'Not true,' said Chris. 'What about Sunday?'

'Oh yes,' remembered Ed, 'except Sundays, that's when we go to chapel. Your family will be there too, only don't get excited because you won't be able to talk to them. We're still separated, with all the boys standing at the front of the chapel. You can tilt your head back to see them, which will give you a stiff neck. Other than Sunday, it's the same every day.'

'Not true,' said Chris. 'What about when we do tasks on the farm?'

'Oh yes,' remembered Ed, 'some days we do tasks on the farm like feeding the pigs or scaring the crows. It's great fun if you like being outdoors – you get to see the animals and run around. Other than that, it's the same every day.'

'Not true.' said Chris. 'What about when you get into trouble?'

By this point Ed had had enough. 'Why don't you tell him if you're so clever?'

'Gladly,' smiled Chris. 'A sure way to break the pattern of your Workhouse day is to get into a right load of trouble. I wouldn't recommend it, oh no, not at all. You might find you end up in the dungeon!'

'The dungeon?' repeated Joe, full of terror.

'Never been there,' said Chris, 'but I've heard it's a small, dark cell with no window, no light and sometimes, they will leave you there for days. Imagine that! Must be very spooky at night time! There was a lady called Honor Dickerson who threw some bread for her son over the yard wall. It was the dungeon for her. They kept her there for a very long time.'

'Oh dear,' said Joe, 'that's sad.'

'Wooooohhhhhh, the dungeeeeeeooooon, ooohhhhhhhh!' Ed suddenly pounced on Joe. It was clearly only meant to give Joe a bit of a playful fright, but he wasn't expecting it and nearly jumped out of his skin.

'Oh sorry!' Ed said sheepishly. 'Didn't mean to make you jump like that.'

Chris nudged him sharply, 'You're so silly!'

Ed nudged him back, 'No, you're so silly!'

'No, you're so silly!'

'No, you're so silly!'

'You're both so silly!' Joe interrupted them. Chris and Ed stared at Joe dumbfounded. Joe grinned. Then the boys started laughing. Joe laughed too, the hardest he had laughed for a very long time. The three laughed and laughed and laughed. Joe had made two very good friends. He was happy about that, true enough.

Having friends made life much easier for Joe and he soon got used to the Workhouse. One day, he was charged with the task of going to the farm alone with a small cart to bring back some milk churns to the Workhouse. It was a bright summer's day. There had been rain the night before which had left many muddy puddles on the farm and he enjoyed steering the cart around them with a spring in his step. It was lovely to hear the birds chirping in the trees and to see the cows in the flowery fields. He was looking forward to school and seeing his friends later that day.

On his way back from the farm, with the little cart loaded with milk churns, Joe found himself feeling all light-hearted. He skipped and sprang in some of the little puddles, the cart whizzing in front of him. Skip, splash, skip, splash! All of a sudden, Joe caught sight of his reflection in one of the puddles on the ground and saw that his hair had fully grown back after it was shaved on his first day. In fact, it had grown so much that it was all floppy. He must have been at the Workhouse for a long time.

Thinking about his first day reminded Joe of how it felt to be separated from his family. Although he had since frequently seen them at Sunday chapel, it wasn't the same as spending time with them. A familiar image flashed through his mind, the image of Lucy getting Nancy taken away. Joe wondered when he would ever give her a cuddle. His heart sank, he stopped skipping, and with the cart trundling in front of him, walked slowly back to the Workhouse.

Years passed until Joe was fourteen, old enough to get a job outside the Workhouse and keen as anything to crack on and make a life for himself. He found out that his mum and dad were now living together in Cherry Tree Cottage, a beautiful cottage on the Workhouse grounds where elderly couples were allowed to live together. Joe was happy that his parents were back together again and felt ready to move on and get a job.

A man at the Workhouse called Mr Keppel assisted boys in finding jobs. Mr Keppel was the Chairman of the Guardians. The Guardians were people who kept the Workhouse in order and made the rules. Joe thought Guardians must be quite strict people, although he had much admiration for Mr Keppel. He thought

Mr Keppel was a very kind man who really went the extra mile to help the likes of him find good jobs outside the Workhouse. He had heard how Mr Keppel had helped a boy to overcome a real obstacle in his life. A boy called George Bales only had one arm, but with the other arm he showed excellent artistic talent, so much talent that Mr Keppel helped to find him a place at art school.

Joe knew that it was unusual for a Guardian to take such interest in securing good futures for Workhouse children and he was grateful for Mr Keppel's help. Joe was eager to be back working in the great outdoors and Mr Keppel found him a job on one of the many local farms. Better yet, Chris and Ed got jobs on the same farm, so Joe would be with his friends.

Whilst excited about moving forward, Joe had to admit he felt sad to be leaving the Workhouse. Life in the Workhouse had been tough, that was true enough; he hadn't been able to spend time with his family, was always being told what to do and had to live with the horrible thought of that frightening dungeon. That said, he felt the Workhouse had given him a better start in life than he would have had if he'd grown up on the farm. Thanks to the Workhouse, he'd had a good education and hadn't gone hungry. He'd made friends and received help from kind people he'd met along the way, like Mr Bradfield, strict but fair, who had taught Joe the three Rs, and Mr Keppel, who worked relentlessly so that Workhouse children stood a real chance of making a life for themselves, a life to be proud of. For this, Joe was extremely grateful.

Overall, it seemed to Joe that while some things had been bad, other things had been good. For every grey sky, there was a silver lining. Joe kept this in mind as he left the Workhouse. He stepped outside that green door with the clenched fist knocker and watched it close. 'Goodbye,' the clenched fist knocker seemed to say, 'you're out now, so stay out!'

Stay out Joe did, and he was glad to. He stayed out and enjoyed his job on the farm alongside Chris and Ed. He stayed out and met a lovely maid called Mary and the two got married. He stayed out and had his first child with Mary, a beautiful baby called Elizabeth. But there was one reason Joe wished he had stayed in and that reason was Lucy. It had been so long since he had seen his sister and he didn't know what had become of her.

Now, one day, Mary heard word of Lucy in the local village and rushed home to tell Joe. Lucy was all grown up and working as a nurse in the Workhouse. Joe could hardly believe it, this was too wonderful – Lucy, a nurse! He couldn't have imagined a better profession for his bright sister. Joe wasn't sure if Lucy would want to hear from him after all this time, but after much encouragement from Mary, he decided to write Lucy a letter inviting her for afternoon tea at 3 o'clock on Sunday.

Joe knew he had the Workhouse to thank for being able to write such a letter. His heart was in his mouth as he posted it. What if she didn't write back? Imagine, then, Joe's delight when he received this letter and read it out loud to Mary as she held his hand:

Dear Joe,

Thank you for your letter. It is lovely to hear from you.

I am very well and enjoy my job as a nurse at the Workhouse. I often visit Mum and Dad, who live happily together at Cherry Tree Cottage.

I would like to meet for tea on Sunday at 3 o'clock.

Yours,

Lucy

Enclosed with the letter, Lucy had sent a gift for baby Elizabeth. It was a peg doll. A peg doll called Nancy.

Joe and his family are made-up characters for the story, but some characters mentioned were real people, listed below. You can find out more about them, as well as the fascinating stories of lots of other Workhouse inmates at Gressenhall Farm and Workhouse.

Workhouse inmates: Honor Dickerson; George Bales, Chairman of the Guardians; Frederick Keppel, school teacher; Robert Bradfield.

8

MATILDA AND THE SNAP DRAGON

INSPIRED BY MUSEUM OF NORWICH AT THE BRIDEWELL

In the Story – A Snap Dragon

Once upon a time, there lived a little girl who was always getting left behind.

The girl's name was Matilda and she lived many hundreds of years ago in a time called the medieval age in Norwich. Matilda was born to a poor family – they would have been called peasants back in those days – and they all lived together in a house so small that everyone shared the same room to sleep in. There was Mum, Dad, Matilda's older sister, Alice, and her older brothers, Peter and John. Matilda was a good deal younger than her three siblings and never got the chance to join in with any of their games. When Alice, John and Peter played together as children she was just a baby, and by the time she was old enough to play with them, they had all moved out of the house and got jobs and homes of their own.

Little Matilda spent much of her time alone in a room which was once filled with the noise, games and laughter of Alice, Peter and John. She even missed the sound of them quarrelling; it would have been better than all this silence. Matilda had a very active imagination and loved to make up games, but since she had no one to play with, she played alone. Her favourite game was to pretend that she was a princess.

She had got the idea from a play she had seen with her family. This play took place every year on a lovely spring day on the streets of Norwich, when everyone got together for a great big party to celebrate Guild Day.

Back then, Guild Day was a very important day and everyone looked forward to it because it was so much fun, with music, dancing and a theatrical performance – a play of St George and the Dragon. This play would be put on by a group of people who called themselves the Guild of Saint George, and the star of the play was the famous Norwich Snap Dragon. Matilda thought the Snap Dragon was a wonderful sight with his scales of red, green and gold. He had a pointy jaw with sharp teeth from which he blew bright flames of fire. When he clamped those toothy jaws together, they went 'snap!' and it made everyone jump. Even though his snappy jaws could be a bit scary, Matilda thought this was all part of the fun, especially when he made everyone jump – it was very funny.

The Snap Dragon wasn't the only performer in the show, there was also a knight in shining armour with a wooden sword – he was Saint George. But as much as Matilda loved to see Saint George and the Snap Dragon, it wasn't these two characters who really captured her imagination. The character she loved best wasn't in the title of the play but was, to her mind, the most magnificent. For Matilda, the real star of the show was the princess.

The princess wore a long, flowing pink dress and a golden crown. Matilda thought the princess was the most fantastic person she had ever seen and she wanted to be just like her. She imagined that if she was a princess, her dress would be made from flowers of every colour of the rainbow all woven together and her crown would be made from sparkling stars. She would surely live somewhere grand surrounded by people. A princess would certainly have lots of people around her and that thought made her feel altogether less lonely. After all, she supposed, princesses were seldom alone because people wanted to be around them so much.

Matilda liked to walk up and down her room pretending that she was taking a stroll through a beautiful garden, surrounded by trees, flowers and, best of all, people. She waved at the people as she passed by and they waved back, bowed or curtsied. But when she stopped imagining, she remembered that she was in her room, alone.

Matilda always looked forward to Guild Day. The arrival of that one day meant that two dreams would come true. One, she could see the princess in the play and, two, she could see all her family again. Mum, Dad, Alice, Peter and John would all be there.

It was the night before the Guild Day celebrations when Matilda saw a brilliant star glistening in the sky. There was nothing particularly unusual about stars in the sky, only this one was so bright that it filled the room with light. Matilda went up to the window and stood on her tiptoes so that she could see out of it properly. She looked up at the beautiful, glowing star. 'Please, oh please, oh please, can I see the princess and my brothers and sister every day!'

The star carried on twinkling and sparkling and Matilda wondered if it had heard her wish at all.

The next day, Matilda was up very early and she, Mum and Dad all headed to Norwich Cathedral which was where the play would take place. The streets were beautifully decorated with many colourful banners and all around bubbled with the hustle and bustle, chatter and singing of people having a jolly time. Matilda felt swept up in the amazing atmosphere; it felt wonderful to have lots of people around when she usually spent so much time alone. She was so excited about seeing the princess that she skipped all the way to Norwich Cathedral while holding Mum's hand.

Norwich Cathedral was an enormous, splendid building with tall turrets which shot all the way up to the clear, blue sky. Outside the entrance to the cathedral, a huge crowd had gathered to watch the play. Matilda began to feel very excited indeed as she saw the Snap Dragon with his toothy snapping jaws and the knight with his shining armour – that meant the princess was close, very close. Oh, but where was she?

Matilda looked all around her, hoping with all her might that she would catch sight of that golden crown sparkling in the sun, but the princess wasn't anywhere to be seen. Matilda felt very sad and disappointed. To make matters worse, it didn't appear as though her siblings were there either. She couldn't see Alice, Peter or John anywhere amongst the crowd.

'Mum,' Matilda tugged at Mum's skirt. 'Where's the princess? And where are Alice, Peter and John?'

'I don't know,' said Mum. 'Where can they be?'

Matilda's heart sank. It seemed that none of her dreams would come true that day. If she couldn't even see the princess or her siblings on Guild Day, she certainly wasn't going to see them every day!

All of a sudden, the Snap Dragon came dancing through the crowd towards her. Everyone watched as he passed them on his way straight to Matilda. Beside the Snap Dragon were Alice, Peter and John. Matilda was very happy to see her siblings, although she was startled that they were heading in her direction with the Snap Dragon. She could hardly believe her eyes. Why was he coming towards her when the play was about to start? She wasn't in the play, now, was she?

'Well, I can't see the princess from the play,' said Mum. 'But I can see a princess right here!'

What happened next was incredible. Alice lifted up Matilda and placed her on the Snap Dragon's back. The next thing Matilda knew, the Snap Dragon was walking in a procession through the crowd and across the street with Matilda on his back. He walked very slowly and gently so that she wouldn't fall off, it was magical feeling as though she were flying through the air. Alice, Peter and John all walked beside her.

'Make way for the princess!' they called to the crowd. 'Make way for Princess Matilda!'

All around her, people bowed and curtsied. Matilda was full of joy, she was a princess, a real princess just like in her imaginary games. She waved at people and they waved back and smiled.

After a while, the Snap Dragon walked back to the entrance of Norwich Cathedral and Alice lifted Matilda down from his back. Then, the real princess, the princess who performed in the play every year with her long, flowing pink dress and golden crown, walked up to Matilda. She had a lovely, warm face with a great big smile and she gave Matilda a little curtsey. 'It's wonderful to meet you, Princess Matilda,' she said, as she curtseyed.

Matilda felt a bit shy about meeting the princess, but she curtseyed back. Then the Snap Dragon, the knight and princess took their places for the play to begin, the play of Saint George and the Dragon. Matilda's family all huddled together to watch and Matilda held Alice's hand. She was so excited about what had happened that although she enjoyed the play she could hardly concentrate. All the while she was thinking that the princess must have known what was going to happen, which was why she stayed hidden until after the Snap Dragon's procession. What's more, her whole family must have got together and planned this – how else could it have happened?

Matilda understood that she wouldn't see the princess or her siblings every day, just as she had wished, but all the same it felt as though her dreams had still come true. She had been surrounded by people, people who cared about her so much that they had planned for her to be a princess. Even if they weren't there all the time, she was never really alone or left behind. From that day on, Alice, Peter and John frequently came to the house to play with Matilda. She

mostly wanted to play princesses because, after all, it is the most terrific fun.

Whenever Matilda felt lonely, she remembered the magical time when she was a princess riding on the Snap Dragon's back and everyone waved, bowed or curtseyed as she passed by. She remembered that day and knew that she was never alone. With this in mind, Matilda would tell you, dreams may not always come true in the way you thought they would, but with a big imagination, lots of love and determination, something even brighter and more beautiful can happen when you make a wish.